Killer Cover Letters and Resumes

Third Edition

By Rosanne Lurie & Selena Welz

WetFeet Insider Guide

WetFeet, Inc.

The Folger Building
101 Howard Street
Suite 300
San Francisco, CA 94105

Phone: (415) 284-7900 or 1-800-926-4JOB
Fax: (415) 284-7910
Website: www.WetFeet.com

Killer Cover Letters and Resumes

Third Edition
By Rosanne Lurie & Selena Welz
ISBN: 1-58207-555-7

Table of Contents

Resumes and Cover Letters at a Glance

The Resume's Raison d'Etre

- 30 seconds or less to get you to the interview room—or not

- Functions as your personal marketing piece

- Shows the recruiter exactly how you fit into the position or company

- Draws a clear line as to where you want to go next

Cover Letters

- Sometimes play a major role, and sometimes do not

- Serve to introduce you to the employer and compel him or her to learn more about you

- Should be as brief and concise as possible, while still inciting interest

- Should compliment your resume, not repeat it

Anatomy of the Resume

- Content: education, experience, other

- Objective/summary of skills: optional; use or omit according to your situation

- Format: clean, clear, conservative

- Avoid: cuteness, colored paper or graphics, lies, or bloated or unclear language

No Ifs, Ands, or Buts

- You must customize your resume to each employer you send it to, or at the very least, each type of job you're pursuing.

- You must address your (customized!) cover letter to a specific person, even if that person is simply the head of HR.

- You must research the industries and employers to which you're applying so that you have a better sense of their needs.

- If emailing your resume, you must paste a text version of it in the body of your email.

Top-Five Characteristics Sought by Employers

1. Communication skills

2. Honesty/integrity

3. Interpersonal skills

4. Strong work ethic

5. Teamwork skills

Telling Your Story

Think about all of the things you've done in your life that prepared you for the career that you're pursuing. But keep in mind that your message needs to be targeted—don't try to tell your entire life story or entire work history. Select only those items that may be of interest to a particular employer.

30 Seconds to Satisfy

Looking Good on Paper

The Bottom Line

Looking Good on Paper

You're ready to begin the job hunt. You know what types of positions and companies you'd like to apply to. Now you just need to whip together a resume and proceed, right? Sounds simple—but writing a resume that raises you above the pack and conveys your perfect fit to an employer is a handsome challenge indeed, especially if you take into account that most recruiters spend an average of 30 seconds scanning a resume before sending it to the "yes" or "no" pile. You've got the goods: experience, education, personality. But how do you sum up a lifetime's worth of hard work and accomplishments in one or two pages of text?

INSIDER TIP

On average, most recruiters spend about 30 seconds scanning a resume before sending it to the "yes" or "no" pile.

The first step to creating killer cover letters and resumes is understanding what they really are and how they should be used in a successful job search. Many people think of cover letters as mere formalities accompanying a resume, full of inflated, impersonal language, and rife with business-speak. The more syllables, the better. Resumes are generally considered documents tracing one's work history and skills. To some degree, this is true. Cover letters are formal accompaniments to resumes, intended to introduce a job candidate, while resumes do indeed explain a portion of one's work history and skills.

But cover letters and resumes are also much more than that. They are an advertisement for a quality product: you. They're marketing tools to get the attention of your desired audience—potential employers—and interest them in learning more about the product—you. How do consumer products companies get us to buy their products? Marketing. How do financial services companies attract more customers? Marketing. How do political candidates move their campaigns forward? That's right, marketing.

In this light, it's easy to see how important a killer cover letter and resume are to a job search—and how much potential these marketing tools have. But any successful marketing campaign requires a carefully crafted message that speaks directly to the needs of its audience. Your resume should make recruiters say, "Yes! This is exactly what we need. I want to meet this candidate to learn more."

"" Most online job postings bury recruiters with literally hundreds of resumes. . . . The ease that job seekers can respond to postings online is now their greatest obstacle. —Mike Worthington of ResumeDoctor.com

Many job seekers make the fundamental mistake of viewing the job search in terms of their own needs and desires. While these are certainly important factors in finding a fulfilling job and career path, it is not the most effective way of approaching employers.

Rather than viewing your target employers from the outside in, look at them from the inside out, and place yourself in the recruiter's shoes. You need to understand what employers look for in the initial review of applications, and what qualities will lead you to the next stage in the hiring process.

This book will show you how to closely look at your own skills and experience, do careful research on your potential employers, and craft a compelling marketing message in the form of a killer cover letter and resume.

To get some sense of the employers' perspective, check out this bit of information: Recently, ResumeDoctor.com contacted more than 5,000 recruiters and hiring managers throughout the United States and Canada regarding the success of using online job postings. More than 92 percent of those surveyed reported being inundated with irrelevant responses to their job postings. Most participants indicated that they receive hundreds of responses per online job posting.

Additional complaints included:

- A majority of resumes do not match the job description. [71%]

- Job seekers "blasting out" unsolicited resumes. [63%]

- Job seekers fail to follow specific resume submission instructions found in job post. [34%]

Mike Worthington of ResumeDoctor.com says, "Most online job postings bury recruiters with literally hundreds of resumes. . . . The ease that job seekers can respond to postings online is now their greatest obstacle."

For more information, visit www.ResumeDoctor.com or see the resource section at the end of this guide.

Did you hear that, folks? The number-one complaint from employers is that most resumes they receive don't match the posted job description—most applicants are not fulfilling the employers' needs, or even trying to. While the high number of responses to job postings may be an obstacle, the lack of preparation (not to mention customization) by most job seekers presents a grand opportunity to the savvy resume writer, soon to be you after reading this guide.

DETERMINING YOUR DIRECTION

A successful job search requires planning and organization. You may be mentally vowing to research employers and career paths, network with all your contacts, send out your prospecting letters, and the like. But the first and foremost step is to take a wide view of your entire work history, skills, personal interests, and life path to determine your overall direction. Your work history should appear as a series of thoughtful steps leading up to the present, rather than a haphazard collection of experiences gained through chance and serendipity. Your path isn't that linear, you say? Then it's your job to carefully select what to feature from your work history and skill set to present an organized picture.

A successful resume presents an employer with a clear path, and in the best cases, a clear path leading right to the employer's job opportunity. To light the way, you'll need detailed knowledge of your own skills and work history, knowledge of the employer to which you're presenting your resume, and of the available job opportunity. If you're simply introducing yourself to an employer to prepare for future opportunities, knowing what the employer may need or want is just as crucial.

INSIDER TIP

To keep your message targeted and successful, be prepared to customize your resume for each employer to which you send it. At the very least, you'll need to present a custom resume for each *type* of job you pursue.

Once you've made a thorough assessment of your own skills and work history, community activities, education, even hobbies, you can judiciously select the most enticing bits to present to a particular employer. And what may be enticing to one employer may not be as appealing to the next—that's why you'll need to know a little something about what an employer may need from you. To keep your message targeted and successful, be prepared to customize your resume for each employer to which you send it. At the very least, you'll need to present a custom resume for each *type* of job you pursue.

From your self-assessment and employer research, you should be able to draw out the corresponding themes—that is, find the connections between your skills and the employer's needs and draw a path between the two. Let's say for example that you're applying for a job as a design director for a magazine, but you've never held this specific position before. You have, however, worked as a print production manager for a publishing company, and a graphic designer for an advertising agency. In college, you minored in visual arts and worked on the student newspaper. You've also volunteered as a docent in the modern art museum and done some additional freelance design work.

At first glance, these might seem like a collection of experiences only tangentially related to a job as a design director. But let's start from the beginning of the path in college. You have hands-on visual arts skills and worked on a fast-paced periodical, the student newspaper. To that, you added experience as a graphic designer, showing that you have first-hand experience in the graphic arts industry, know how to put designs together in a real-world context, and have used design in marketing endeavors for the ad agency. Your volunteer work as a docent at the modern art museum highlights your personal interest in the visual arts, particularly modern art, which has the closest relation to current graphic design. Your freelance graphic design work shows that you have the ability to manage graphic projects from concept to completion, not to mention an entrepreneurial bent. And finally, you've proven that you can manage both projects and other workers with your experience as a production manager. This chain of experiences draws a reasonable path to a role as a design director for a print periodical. The experiences may not have been sequential, but the way in which you present them can still clearly show how you would fit into the new role.

What about entry-level candidates without much work experience? The same rules apply, but you'll need to draw from your education, extracurricular activities, volunteer or community work, and personal interests. Altogether, the skills, experience, and interests you present should clearly point to the job opportunity as the natural next step in your progression.

This may seem like an overwhelming task if you're just getting started. But don't worry—we'll take you through the process step by step.

For starters, you'll learn about the best ways to prepare for your job search, including how to determine and articulate your strengths, research techniques, and how to customize your presentation toward desired positions and organizations. Next, you'll get the full scoop on how to create a killer resume and cover letter—from what information it should (and shouldn't) contain to how it should look and sound. Multiple cover letter and resume examples, as well as suggestions for creating layouts that suit your unique needs, will give you great ideas for how your own materials should come together. The section on special concerns examines common problem areas—such as international careers, "overqualified" candidate syndrome, or big time gaps—with helpful suggestions for addressing them. The final section contains suggestions for following up your application, as well as resources that will help you in your job search.

INSIDER TIP

In a nutshell, your cover letter and resume are less about where you have been than about where you want to go next.

The Bottom Line

At best, resume readers spend 30 seconds reviewing a cover letter or resume the first time. This is especially true in a competitive job market, where recruiters may receive up to 200 responses to a single advertised job posting. In 30 seconds, your cover letter and resume package needs to convey an image of who you are, what you're capable of, and how you've used your abilities to achieve specific results. Ideally, it indicates that you know yourself well and have a firm grasp on what you bring to the table. In a nutshell, your cover letter and resume are less about where you have been than about where you want to go next.

Although insiders tell us "there isn't one right answer" to the question of how to create a good cover letter or resume (phew!), they say that the best materials are concise, results-oriented, and very clearly presented. Of course, a great resume alone won't land you the job of your dreams, but appropriate choices in shaping your materials make you far more likely to get a call, and can even help you sail more smoothly through the interview process. This guide will show you the way.

On Your Mark, Get Set, Prep!

Determining What You Have to Offer

Analyzing Your Skills

Building Your Skills List

Determining What You Have to Offer

Ever get stuck watching Uncle Fred's travel slides? Time ticks mercilessly by as Fred displays endless photos while giving blow-by-blow descriptions of people you will never meet and places you'd never want to visit. Whatever you do, do not let your cover letter and resume become like Uncle Fred's pictures. Always keep your audience in mind, and include only the highlights of your experiences.

Before you begin writing, have a good look at yourself. Which elements of your years of wisdom, experience, and accomplishment belong on a couple of sheets of paper, and which don't? What characteristics make you stand out from the crowd but also show that you're a team player? What kind of candidate does your target employer usually hire? Be prepared to think through your activities and achievements and tell your compelling life story in one to two pages.

In addition to knowing all of the factual information about yourself—including grades, test scores, and dates of employment—think about how to portray yourself in a positive, confident light while telling the true story of who you are and what you've accomplished. You must have insight into your strengths and weaknesses to create a compelling letter and resume.

Get started by cataloguing all of your knowledge areas, skills sets, and abilities. No need to get fancy here, just brainstorm and create a comprehensive list. Your knowledge areas will be drawn from your education, past employment, vocational training, or certifications. Your skills and abilities, however, are developed through a variety of life experiences. Following are the main areas to look at when listing your skills and abilities.

EMPLOYMENT HISTORY

The best way to get started with any resume is to map out your employment history. Previous experience in areas similar or related to the position being filled is the first thing any employer will look for when evaluating a potential candidate.

Prepare a chronological list of the major jobs you've held. Include the company names, your titles, managers' names, the time you spent in those positions, starting and ending salaries, and primary responsibilities.

This will give you a good foundation to start building the basic content of your resume. But just as important, seeing your work history laid out will help you identify upward trends in your career, such as responsibility, increasing salary, or other advancement. Your employment history will also reveal any gaps that you'll need to account for on the resume or in the interview.

OTHER TYPES OF EXPERIENCE

Entry-level candidates won't have much experience in the kind of position for which they're applying. Or they may have very little work experience at all. Career changers face the same dilemma when applying for a new type of job.

If either of these is the case for you, look to other sources of inspiration when mapping out your past experience.

Academic Study

Review your school curriculum and make note of any special areas of study. What was your major? Did you have a minor? Did you take any special courses, such as business communication, economics, media, or art history? These areas of knowledge may be helpful in applying for certain jobs.

While you're at it, gather your school transcripts, standardized test scores, scholarship applications and awards, and any other information that may help you paint a picture of your academic capability. Calculate your GPA, because you might need this information at some point. If you're concerned about your GPA, calculate it using several cuts—overall, major-only, or by year—to see which provides the most favorable view to note on your resume, or at least mention in the interview if asked. Always use a standard 4.0 scale.

Volunteer or Community Activities

Volunteering is a great way to gain valuable experience that can be applied to a job. Make note of any community activities in which you've participated. Volunteer as a Big Brother or Big Sister? Part of the Rotary Club? Deliver meals during the holidays? All of these activities can be sources of valuable experience to present to an employer. Not only that, but extracurricular activities such as these also tell the employer something about your motivation, character, values, and work ethic.

For entry-level candidates without a lot of work experience, volunteering is a great way to get some experience!

Academic or Professional Organizations

Extracurricular activities, whether academic or professional, are another great way to present valuable nonprofessional experience. Make note of any organizations you are or have been involved in and note the role you played in each. Again, entry-level candidates and career changers can use these to leverage their application for a new position, so if you haven't been involved in anything like this, now is the time!

Top Accomplishments

List the most significant accomplishments from your professional, academic, and personal experiences. Write down each achievement; then explain why it is significant to you, how you achieved it, how others helped you, and how you measure its success. You will need to include information about at least two of your top accomplishments in your resume, preferably with an indication of the results achieved.

Analyzing Your Skills

Every job seeker has a variety of professional and personal experience to draw from when identifying and articulating his or her skills and abilities. Look beyond just your work history when listing what you have to offer in your next job. A career is developed through a accumulation of life experiences, both in and outside of the workplace.

"HARD" VS "SOFT" SKILLS

Many employers and recruiters separate professional skills into two sets: "hard" skills and "soft" skills. Hard skills typically include the more left-brained areas, such as programming, mechanical aptitude, finance, accounting, marketing, operations, and strategy. Soft skills are the right-brained areas such as communication, interpersonal skills, collaboration, leadership, motivation, and creativity. The soft skill set has, in the past, suffered derision at the hands of employers, being ranked below the mighty hard skill set that defined the Information Age (all those humanities majors out there can probably relate). But in today's employment market, the soft skills are gaining a whole new respect.

Employers responding to an annual survey conducted by the National Association of Colleges and Employers (NACE) ranked communication skills, honesty and integrity, interpersonal skills, work ethic, and teamwork—all soft skills—at the top of their list of desired qualities in a candidate. In fact, communication skills are ranked as the number-one candidate quality desired by employers year after year. And how often do you see "strong communication skills" and "ability to work in teams" listed on job postings? Chances are that you've seen this a lot, indicating that employers across industries really do want these soft skills in candidates.

This is not to say, however, that the hard skills aren't just as important. Most successful people display a balance of both skill sets. So, to escape the value judgment inherent in describing these as "hard" and "soft" skills, let's recast them as "functional" and "strate-gic" skills instead. A successful resume displays a reasonable balance of both areas.

This presents challenges to job candidates with technical backgrounds and humanities backgrounds alike. Those applying for technical positions need to include some empha-sis on strategic skills, such as teamwork and communication, while those applying for non-technical positions would benefit from including some level of analytical ability, such as marketing, finance, or computer skills.

ABILITIES AND TALENTS

Abilities and talents offer a whole other area of inspiration when planning your resume. Skills are distinct sets of learned knowledge whereas abilities, or talents, are inherent— and these usually point us to the kind of jobs for which we should apply, and at which we'll probably be happiest and most successful. So, don't forget to incorporate your tal-ents and natural abilities in your list of skills.

Good at making friends? Then your interpersonal skills must be top-notch! Great at last-minute Halloween costumes? Then you must be highly visually creative! Never read assembly instructions? Then you must have superior mechanical aptitude! Be sure to pay attention to the things you're good at, because you probably use them in your cur-rent job or other activities all the time. And they probably help shape your most valu-able professional attributes.

ENTRY-LEVEL CANDIDATES: "BOTTOM-LINE" SKILLS

Entry-level and internship candidates are especially challenged when it comes to prov-ing their mettle to potential employers because most don't have much significant work experience behind them. But rest assured, the top qualities that most employers want have nothing to do with work experience or education. Take a look at some recent data from the National Association of Colleges and Employers (NACE):

- Employers responding to NACE's *Job Outlook 2005* survey were asked to rate the importance of candidate qualities and skills on a five-point scale, with five being "extremely important" and one being "not important." Communication skills (4.7 average), honesty/integrity (4.7), interpersonal skills (4.5), strong work ethic (4.5), and teamwork skills (4.5) were the most desired characteristics.

- Employers consistently rank these skills at the top of their lists year after year.

- The majority of the respondents to this survey (45.7 percent) were service-sector employers; 40.5 percent were manufacturers, and 13.8 percent were government/ non-profit employers.

To find out more about the *NACE Job Outlook 2005* survey, please see the resource section at the end of this guide, or visit www.naceweb.org.

Effective self-promotion begins with understanding an employer's vision of an attractive candidate. Your cover letter and resume must communicate your ability to deliver the desired goods. Fortunately, all of the qualities mentioned above can be shown through education, extracurricular and community activities, or special projects.

IDENTIFYING TRANSFERABLE SKILLS

The following section reviews employers' most sought-out attributes in a broad spectrum of industries. Which skills you choose to highlight depends on the particular require-ments of the position and the corporate culture of each company you're targeting. The list of questions following each skill set will help you identify your relevant skills and what you've accomplished with them. These questions should also help you see that skills or expertise developed in one context can help you prepare for a successful career in another.

Quantitative and Analytical Ability

Quantitative or analytical skills are critical components of many jobs, particularly in business and scientific fields. They are fundamental to your success in industries such as financial services and consulting, especially during the first few years of your career. In these fields, if you show no evidence of these skills, you will not get to the interview.

Have you:

- Filtered through data and assumptions and identified reasonable responses to complex problems?

- Synthesized large amounts of information and identified issues?

- Identified a problem and taken a proactive approach to solving it?

- Done well in courses with heavy analytical and quantitative content?

- Performed experiments that required formulation of a hypothesis and collection of evidence to prove or disprove it?

- Taken courses in mathematics, statistics, or other subjects that utilize analytical thinking?

If so, you may have the quantitative or analytical ability employers look for.

Drive for Results (Initiative)

An increasing number of companies and nonprofit organizations are emphasizing results in describing their hiring needs. Employers in any field want to know whether you have the ambition, motivation, attention to detail, and energy necessary to deliver real results.

Have you:

- Brought new customers or revenue into your company? Developed new programs or initiatives?

- Proven that you're a self-starter who goes above and beyond requirements?

- Shown the ability to switch priorities and move quickly among different tasks?

- Set a challenging goal and achieved it?

- Attended to the details while juggling multiple tasks?

- Taken an innovative and/or efficient approach to getting something done?

The need for specific, quantitative measurements of your accomplishments should start you thinking about how to track and measure your achievements if you don't do that already.

Achievement/Intellectual Capacity

Are you outstanding in any of your accomplishments? Employers may be interested in people who can achieve beyond the norm, or who can demonstrate ambition in their endeavors.

Have You:

- Earned honors or academic awards?

- Received academic scholarships or fellowships?

- Taken on challenging courses or a heavy workload?

- Pursued intellectual activities (chess, computer programming, etc.)?

- Attended academically rigorous schools?

- Done well on standardized tests (SAT, GMAT, LSAT, and so on)?

- Earned a high GPA?

- Received awards and recognition in the workplace?

Leadership

Leadership can be expressed both through your managerial experience and through your willingness to take on responsibility, even if your role is not that of a supervisor or team captain. Many employers look for leadership qualities in their staff.

Have you:

- Managed people?

- Facilitated meetings?

- Led teams in solving problems?

- Coordinated outside vendors?

- Held a leadership position in a school organization, team, or club?

- Been elected to a post by your peers?

- Organized or coordinated significant events?

- Had a position of significant responsibility with a previous employer?

- Hired or fired anyone?

Teamwork

Teamwork with clients and/or colleagues is a critical component of most work environments. Employers look for people who can work effectively with others and inspire them toward a common goal. This means an ability to communicate clearly and collaboratively with managers, peers, assistants, clients, vendors, and anyone you will have contact with through your work.

Have You:

- Been a member of a sports team, study group, or committee?

- Worked effectively with people whose work style or cultural background differs from yours?

- Inspired others to take action in an unstructured situation?

- Taken on the role of a team leader or player as needed?

Of course, you have. We don't know of any candidate, particularly one with a high level of academic training, who hasn't been involved in working with a team. (Gotta love those study groups!) Identify the teams and/or groups you've been a part of and think about the role you typically play. Employers may want to hear about your ability to make productive contributions, the type of role you tend to play on a team, or how you've worked with a team to identify and solve a problem.

Industry and Functional Expertise

If you have a strong understanding of an industry though experience or academic training, highlight this in your cover letter and resume. Of course, the skills that are considered most important very by industry. Here are some useful ways to think about your knowledge and past exposure.

Have you:

- Worked in a particular industry for a good chunk of time?

- Held various roles within one industry?

- Held similar functional roles in different industries? Been able to apply your functional knowledge from one industry to another?

- Written a thesis or research paper about a particular industry, business issue, or other topic?

- Volunteered in a particular field, or followed current events related to an industry or issue?

- Participated in conventions, conferences, symposiums, or associations in a specific field?

- Developed specialized skills—such as technical, industry-based, administrative, or in-depth knowledge from your academic training?

Unlike Uncle Fred, with his approach to sharing past exploits, you can carefully develop focused descriptions of the most interesting and valuable of your experiences to share with recruiters and hiring managers. The goal of assessing your skills is being able to identify what you can offer an employer, and demonstrate how hiring you will help a company meet its objectives.

Building Your Skills List

Review the following list of skills and circle or highlight the competencies you've demonstrated in your work, academic, or personal experiences. The categories in which they're organized represent some of the major core skill areas sought by employers. These "action" words will form the basis of your achievement statements, discussed in the next chapter. Use the extra spaces to write down additional skills for each of the various categories.

Communication	Teamwork	Managerial
authored	assisted	administered
composed	backed	approved
consulted	brokered	conducted
conveyed	collaborated	decided
corresponded	contributed	delegated
drafted	cooperated	directed
edited	coordinated	executed
explained	helped	guided
finessed	participated	handled
interpreted	partnered with	hired
justified	reinvigorated	managed
mediated	shared	oversaw

negotiated	solidified	project managed
reported	strategized	ran
revised	supported	regulated
simplified	synergized	supervised
translated	united	trained
Leadership	**Initiative**	**Adaptability**
coached	achieved	adapted
conducted	conceived	adopted
enabled	created	anticipated
facilitated	cultivated	changed
founded	designed	complied
governed	determined	engineered
guided	developed	improved
headed	devised	integrated
instructed	established	invented
led	expanded	learned
motivated	garnered	mastered
piloted	generated	modified
prescribed	implemented	negotiated
recommended	initiated	problem solved
taught	instituted	resolved
unified	launched	retrenched
united	originated	trained

Analytical	Organizational	Results/Achievements
analyzed	administered	built
appraised	arranged	completed
assessed	compiled	doubled/tripled
broke down	coordinated	grew
calculated	distributed	made
categorized	gathered	outpaced
evaluated	operated	produced
examined	ordered	rebuilt
experimented	organized/reorganized	reduced
innovated	maintained	reenergized
inspected	managed	sold
investigated	prepared	solved
quantified	prioritized	started up
researched	processed	transformed
reviewed	scheduled	maximized/minimized
surveyed	sequenced	turned around
systemized	synthesized	won over

The Recipe for Resume Success

It's How You Say It: Use of Language

Your Basic Resume Ingredients

It's How You Say It: Use of Language

When it comes to resume writing, there is a specific use of language to keep in mind. For those of you who may feel insecure about your writing—fear not. Using language effectively in a resume is challenging, but by keeping a few basic rules and principles in mind, any literate person can do it.

You'll never fit everything you want to say onto a one- or two-page resume. That means that you need to carefully select what you're going to say, but also be conscientious of how you say it. In a format such as a resume with limited space, you need to choose powerful, effective words that will get your message across immediately. You need to be as specific as possible, leaving no room for questions in a recruiter's mind. And you need to be concise and get to your point quickly. Distill everything you want to say into a selection of carefully chosen words, sentences, and bullet points, so that someone reading your resume can see your accomplishments at a moment's glance, and most importantly, be impressed by them. Careful, concise, powerful language is the only way to achieve this goal.

So let's begin with the basic principles to keep in mind as you're crafting your resume statements.

KEEP IT SIMPLE, SILLY

When it comes to crafting your resume statements, less is more. Keep in mind that you're trying to make your resume as readable as possible by keeping it visually simple with plenty of white space to ease the eyes down the page. Blocks of text and complex, meandering sentences confound scanning for essential information and will only frustrate a recruiter, causing them to set your resume aside and move on to the next one. So keep your sentences simple and make only one carefully chosen point with each one.

This example sentence is trying to say too much:

- Gained new accounts by developing and maintaining relationships with key decision makers in various markets generating $1.7 million revenue in the form of online subscriptions.

It works much better when broken out into two shorter points:

- Increased client base by 20% in the community college, university, and vocational school markets.

- Generated $1.7 million in revenue through new accounts.

AVOID BLOAT

With the goal of crafting simple, clear resume statements, avoid bloated language at all costs. Don't try to impress recruiters with two-bit words and trendy business jargon. Your statements and achievements should be well chosen enough to speak for themselves, without relying on fancy rhetoric to boost their value. Even entry-level candidates with little work experience can craft impressive resume statements based on non-work activities or achievements. That's why what you choose to prioritize and state in your resume is so important.

This sentence needs an antacid:

- Strategized and enacted superior implementation systems and procedures to leverage increased results of positive residential client base feedback, instituting a resulting increase of 100%.

The straightforward approach is usually much more impressive:

- Developed streamlined in-home installation process reducing customer complaints by half.

BE SPECIFIC

Never use general terms to describe your experience or achievements. After all, you're trying to stand out from all the other candidates, not blend in with them. Be as concrete and specific as you can in all of your statements. Use numbers and hard facts wherever possible. Don't say, "managed many important client accounts," say, "managed 30 accounts averaging more than $200k each." In order to evaluate your qualifications for a specific job, the recruiter needs a clear picture of what you've actually done. She needs to be able to visualize your accomplishments. Using fuzzy descriptors such as "some," "many," and "very" will not accomplish this.

This statement is pretty vague:

- Logged daily customer inquiries and forwarded them to appropriate personnel.

Watch how adding a little detail can turn a basic responsibility into an achievement:

- Maintained company's customer-focused reputation by processing 30–40 detailed inquiries daily, managing inquiry routing and prioritization.

USE THE ACTIVE VOICE

Yes, you've heard this before, especially you recent college graduates. Never saw the purpose? Well, being able to craft a powerful resume is one of the benefits of mastering the active voice. Not only is the active voice more effective and forceful, making you the direct subject of your statements, rather than the object (who is having something done to it), but using the active voice also avoids excessive wordiness and helps to keep statements brief, clear, and simple.

This statement makes it sound as if the candidate just stumbled onto a promotion:

- Selected as interim supervisor for 10–12 employees.

A simple rewording of the statement gives the candidate much more credit for the activity:

• Managed 10–12 employees as summer interim supervisor.

WRITE IN THE FIRST PERSON

Your resume is a direct statement from you to a recruiter or potential employer. Therefore, all of your statements need to be written from the first person point-of-view. Using first-person statements also helps ensure the active voice. In the name of saving space and preventing wordiness, however, remove the "I" from your statements.

This summary statement is still clear, even without the "I":

Marketing professional with 7 years experience; specialize in research and strategy development for government- and privately funded organizations; earned community service award through accomplishments in nonprofit fund-raising.

REMOVE ARTICLES AND HELPING VERBS

To further tighten your resume writing, remove any articles (a, an, the) and helping verbs (have, had, may, might, and forms of "to be": am, is, are, was, were) from your resume statements. These extra words can be assumed by the reader, and this is standard resume protocol.

All of the helping verbs make this statement too long:

• Assisted the faculty of the Engineering Department with its research for publications in academic journals.

This revision is much slicker:

• Assisted Engineering Department with research published in various academic journals.

KEEP TRACK OF TENSE

Make sure to describe your past duties and achievements in the past tense, and your present duties and achievements in the present tense. For example, if you're listing your accomplishments at your current job, describe those in the present, immediate sense, not the past sense. Illogical use of tense is confusing, and just plain sloppy. Some job seekers hold two jobs simultaneously or hold an occasional long-term side job along with their full-time job. If you still hold the job, list that in the present tense as well.

This example keeps track of proper verb tense from a past to a present job:

Nov. 2003–present   **Account Manager**, Millburg Group

- Manage sales incentive program comprising 200 retailers with 300+ employee participants.

- Oversee marketing strategy for agency's biggest client (Krandle Motors); helped client achieve 2 consecutive years of record new product sales.

- Develop program marketing materials; 20% new client acquisition by second quarter of 2005.

Aug. 2000–Feb. 2003   **Marketing Manager, Special Programs**, LockSpeed Marketing Group

- Managed creation, production, and implementation of new client incentive program; new clients included 12 Fortune 500 corporations.

- Helped sales force achieve 35% higher sales volume through support tools, methodologies, and proposals.

- Implemented corporate PR strategies, increasing publicity by 20% and securing multiple industry awards, including Best Creative Agency in Southern California.

PROOFREAD, AND PROOFREAD AGAIN

Typos, misspellings, and grammar errors are death on your resume or cover letter. You can never proofread either one too many times. Once you've written up a final draft of your resume, proofread it. Then set it aside for a time (a few hours or days) and proofread it again. Then send it to a few friends and have them proof it. Then proofread it again. . . . you get the picture.

Your Basic Resume Ingredients

Three ingredients that should always appear on every resume are contact information, experience, and education. Other sections, such as an objective statement, summary of qualifications, a profile, activities, additional skills, or interests are optional and should be selected in a manner that best demonstrates how your qualifications fit with the position you're targeting. We'll discuss each of these sections in more detail and when and how they should be used throughout this chapter.

CREATE A RESUME MASTER LIST

Every good cook knows that, unless you're baking a triple-tier layer cake with buttercream frosting, no recipe is exact. Various factors will affect the outcome of a dish: temperature of the day, available ingredients, cooking utensils, spices, prep time available, or the palates of your guests. The same can be said for using your resume and cover letter in the job search. There is no magic formula that will be effective in every given situation.

If you plan on having a successful job search, get comfortable early on with the idea that you'll need to customize your resume for each position to which you apply. One standard resume will simply not work. At the very least, you'll want to create several versions of your resume—one for each *type* of position or industry you're targeting.

Step one is to create a resume master list that includes all of the resume elements that you might use, as well as a full selection of refined achievement statements, coursework, volunteer activities, hobbies, or anything else you might use for a particular job application. This will help you keep all of your resume ingredients in one place. Then, when you're ready to apply for a job, you can simply pick out the elements and achievements from your master list that you think will be most impressive to the employer.

This doesn't mean you need to write a novel here. You still need to carefully craft your statements and pair down the language for maximum effect. But once you've done the work, creating a custom resume for each job application will be a breeze!

Take a look at the following two sample resumes. This applicant has experience in both sales and human resources and is looking for a job in either area. Note how the choice of achievements listed and some creative reworking of job titles places the resume's emphasis on one or the other area. Trying to combine emphasis on both areas in one document would be too confusing and result in a muddled message. This candidate simply pulled out his resume master list and selected his pre-drafted statements to create two customized resumes.

Manuel Rigisio

991 Sunny Street, #35 ◆ Charlotte, NC 28226 ◆ 252.555.7777 ◆ address@email.com

OBJECTIVE

To secure a human resources position that will draw on my core skills, experience, and customer focus to recruit top talent and foster solid business relationships.

PROFESSIONAL STRENGTHS

◆ Networking and Relationship Development	◆ Integrity	◆ Business Analytics
◆ Initiative/Self-Motivator	◆ Efficient Problem Solver	◆ Change Agent

PROFESSIONAL EXPERIENCE

Recruitment Management, Inc., Charlotte, NC   03/03 to present
Recruitment Consultant

Continually strengthen knowledge of current trends in recruitment. Manage sales process from lead generation to close for recruitment management system, recruitment research, and recruitment marketing products. Attended SHRM, EMA, and Spring ERExpo (Electronic Recruiting Exchange) conferences.

Accomplishments:
- ◆ Fastest on-boarded client in company history

Anderson Labs, Boston, MA   04/01 to 02/03
Pharmaceutical Sales Representative

Managed a customer base of 150 physicians. Mentored new hires within district and assisted district manager with recruitment and interviewing. Facilitated and presented product sales' meeting presentations for district.

Accomplishments:
- ◆ 2002 Region Diversity Coordinator—appointed by Region Business Director
- ◆ 2001 Region Leadership Advisory Council—elected by peers
- ◆ District Impact Award Winner—Q1 2002
- ◆ District & Region Synergy Award Winner—Q2, Q3 2002
- ◆ Region Top Performance Club—June, July, September 2002

Enterprise Retail Group, Boston, MA   06/98 to 04/01
Generalist, Human Resources

Primary HR contact for 6 departments: managed employment and recruitment (exempt and non-exempt positions), defused and handled employee relations issues, administered performance appraisals and corrective counseling. Managed all college recruitment activities (10 core campuses).

Accomplishments:
- ◆ 2001 Greater Boston Corporate Junior Achiever—voted by senior management
- ◆ Conceptualized, structured, and managed the corporate office's management training program
- ◆ Certified corporate trainer for the *Diversity Awareness, Diversity Leadership*, and *Retail and Merchandising 101* professional development courses

ERD Group, Inc., Executive Development Program, Boston, MA   06/98 to 01/00
Manager, Credit Customer Service   02/99 to 01/00
- ◆ Managed all aspects of day-to-day operations for 100-person call center staff.
- ◆ Evaluated departmental best practices and audited consistency of procedures across 3 facilities.

Executive Board Presentation   01/99
- ◆ Developed, researched, and proposed a process of change to the ERD Executive Board.
- ◆ Rated #1/15 presentations—evaluated on initiative, research, and overall delivery.

Manager, Retirement Benefits   06/98 to 02/99
- ◆ Managed audits of 401(k) savings plan payments and loans to ensure compliance and accuracy.
- ◆ Project manager for 1998 401(k) 70½ distributions.

EDUCATION

Boston University, Boston, MA   06/98
B.S., Industrial Engineering and Management Sciences
National Society of Professional Engineers:
- ◆ National Executive Board Member—04/97 to 04/98

Manuel Rigisio

991 Sunny Street, #35 ◆ Charlotte, NC 28226 ◆ 252.555.7777 ◆ address@email.com

OBJECTIVE

To secure a medical device sales position that will draw on my core skills, experience, and customer focus to achieve exceptional sales results and foster solid business relationships.

PROFESSIONAL EXPERIENCE

Recruitment Management, Inc., Charlotte, NC   03/03 to present
Sales Manager

Manage sales process from lead generation to close for recruitment management system, recruitment research, and recruitment marketing products. National sales responsibility. Continually strengthen knowledge of current trends in recruitment.

Accomplishments:
- ◆ Fastest close in company history (2 weeks)
- ◆ Continuous management of pipeline with value over $1M
- ◆ Responsible for over 60% of new clients
- ◆ 4 consecutive quarters exceeding quota (total sales over $675K)

Anderson Labs, Boston, MA   04/01 to 02/03
Pharmaceutical Sales Representative

Managed a customer base of 150 physicians with varied specialties: emergency medicine, GI, internal medicine, oto-laryngology, and primary care. Promoted 3 strategic growth products in CNS (psychosis and Alzheimer's disease) and gastroenterology. District coordinator for 1 promoted product. Mentored new hires within district and assisted district manager with recruitment and interviewing. Facilitated and presented product sales' meeting presentations for district. Led district conference calls on business analytics.

Accomplishments:
- ◆ Ranked #1/4 in district, #2/24 in region, and #26/500 in nation—01/03
- ◆ 10 consecutive months of sales growth—04/02 to 02/03
- ◆ #1/500 market share and YTD growth—02/02
- ◆ 6 consecutive months over 200% to quota—09/01 to 02/03
- ◆ Top 10% of national sales force—10/01 to 02/03
- ◆ 2002 Region Diversity Coordinator—appointed by Region Business Director
- ◆ District Impact Award Winner—Q1 2002
- ◆ District & Region Synergy Award Winner—Q2, Q3 2002

Enterprise Retail Group, Boston, MA   06/98 to 04/01
Generalist, Human Resources

Primary HR contact for 6 departments: managed employment and recruitment (exempt and non-exempt positions), defused and handled employee relations issues, administered performance appraisals and corrective counseling. Managed all college recruitment activities.

Accomplishment:
- ◆ 2001 Greater Boston Corporate Junior Achiever—voted by senior management

ERD Group, Inc., Executive Development Program, Boston, MA   06/98 to 01/00
Manager, Credit Customer Service   02/99 to 01/00
- ◆ Evaluated departmental best practices and audited consistency of procedures across 3 facilities.

Executive Board Presentation   01/99
- ◆ Rated #1/15 presentations—evaluated on initiative, research, and overall delivery.

Manager, Retirement Benefits   06/98 to 02/99
- ◆ Managed audits of 401(k) savings plan payments and loans to ensure compliance and accuracy.
- ◆ Project manager for 1998 401(k) 70½ distributions.

EDUCATION

Boston University, Boston, MA   06/98
B.S., Industrial Engineering and Management Sciences
   National Society of Professional Engineers:
   - ◆ National Executive Board Member—04/97 to 04/98

As you're reading through the following descriptions of common resume ingredients, begin jotting down notes on each section to see where you have the most material. From there, pare down your statements to create your master list.

CONTACT INFORMATION

Your name and contact information are the most important things to supply to an employer, and should head the pages of all resumes. Seems straightforward, but many people make the mistake of sending resumes with old contact information, or omitting telephone numbers and email addresses.

Be sure to include the name you use professionally, a home address, and the telephone number or numbers where you are most easily reached. Get an email account if you don't already have one; many employers prefer this method of reaching candidates, including those in nontechnical fields. Stick with a standard email address though. While something like hotbarebackrider@yourmail.com might be fun to use with your friends, it is unprofessional and inappropriate to use in a business setting. Many email programs, such as Yahoo, HotMail, and Gmail are free and easy to sign up for. Just open a new account for your job search if your current email address is a bit too, let's say, imaginative, for use with potential employers.

Most resumes emphasize the applicant's name by placing it in bold or enlarged font. This is a nice way to help break up the space of your resume and present a hierarchy of information. And your ultimate goal is to make your name stand out and stick in the recruiter's mind. Remember that this is a marketing piece about you, and those subtle visual tricks can be very effective. However, don't go crazy by using a ridiculously huge font. Stick with something between 12- and 18-points for the most effective visual punch. And, unless you're a designer and really know what you're doing, stay away from the super fancy fonts, undershadowing, or cutesy decorative symbols. These tricks are unnecessary and tend to look rather juvenile. A row of bullets or simple horizontal line should be the extent of your graphic experimentation in your resume.

Keep your name and contact information positioned in the center or right margin of your heading. This will make it better stand out if it is filed in a folder or binder.

And finally, use the same heading on your cover letter that you have designed for your resume. This looks cleaner and more professional, and serves as a visual cue that the two documents belong together. (And don't forget the visual punch of "branding" your name; a consistent look is much more effective.)

OBJECTIVE STATEMENT

An objective statement is a good way to clarify and convey your immediate career goals and reason for contacting an employer. Professionals with many years of experience in a particular career path who are applying for a job similar to one they've held may skip the objective statement, instead allowing their experience to speak for itself and including one or two extra achievement statements (described in detail later in this chapter). Candidates from more conservative or traditional fields, such as financial services or consulting, should also leave out the objective statement. These fields have standard hiring channels. Submitting your resume is enough to state your objective in these situations. (For more detailed information on investment banking or consulting resumes, see the WetFeet Insider Guides *Killer Investment Banking Resumes!* and *Killer Consulting Resumes!*, both available from www.WetFeet.com)

For all the rest, an objective statement might be effective in the following situations:

- You are applying to a very large company with many similar positions.

- You are an entry-level candidate with little job experience.

- You are a career changer applying for a job in a field in which you have little or no prior experience.

- You are applying for a job that is a clear advancement from those you previously held.

- Your work history consists of a variety of types of experience.

In any case, your objective statement should be specific and straightforward, and limited to one or two concise sentences. Don't bother with the general one-size-fits-all objective statements, such as "I am seeking a challenging position that utilizes and expands my professional skills." That tells the reader nothing and is simply a waste of space. Instead, use the objective statement to customize your resume directly to the job or company that you're applying to. It can be as simple as, "Seeking an associate copywriter position in the advertising industry." Career changers or those trying to emphasize their transferable skills might say something like, "Looking to put my extensive customer service and relationship-building skills to work as a public relations account manager." A well-crafted objective can function as a thesis statement, setting the direction in which the resume will follow.

WRITING AN OBJECTIVE STATEMENT

Part I

Write down the kinds of positions, types of organizations or settings, and specific skills you want to use or develop in your next job.

Position Desired: _____

Setting: _____

Skills or Goals: _____

_____

_____

_____

Part II

Now practice putting the information generated in Part I of this exercise into objective statements you can use in your resume or cover letter. Below are some suggested phrases to get you started.

Seeking a challenging _____ position in the _____ field,

that offers an opportunity to _____.

_____

_____

WRITING AN OBJECTIVE STATEMENT

To use my _____, _____, and _____

skills in a position as a _____.

_____

_____

A career position that would build on my experiences as _____,

while contributing to _____.

_____

_____

Seeking an entry-level opportunity in _____.

_____

_____

To provide _____ to an organization that _____.

_____

_____

SUMMARY OF SKILLS

Including a bulleted list of skills and qualifications near the top of your resume can grab a recruiter's attention and draw him into the details of your experience listed below it. This section can also be titled "Relevant Skills," "Highlight of Qualifications," "Qualifications," "Core Expertise," or any similar variation. Since most recruiters only spend a few seconds scanning a resume before deciding to pass or look more closely, a brief, bulleted list of your strongest points and those most relevant to the job for which you're applying may be the difference between landing in the "yes" or the "no" pile.

 INSIDER TIP

Candidates from financial services and consulting fields should avoid including the objective statement or summary of skills in their resumes.

Highlight sections most benefit job seekers whose qualifications don't exactly match the job description. You're more likely to get the recruiter's attention by emphasizing your transferable skills and exceptional accomplishments at the top of your resume instead of scattering them throughout and expecting the recruiter to connect the dots. As with the objective statement, financial services and consulting candidates can leave this section out.

Your summary statements should be just that: summarizations. Quick, one-line sound bytes that will help your reader identify your most relevant qualifications. An effective summary of skills might cover these bases:

- Number of years' experience in the field or line of work

- Relevant credentials or training

- An accomplishment that directly relates to the job you're applying for

- A personal quality or characteristic that relates to the job (optional)

- Another accomplishment or characteristic that relates to the job (optional)

Don't worry if your cover letter reiterates some of the information in your highlights section. In fact, consider using the cover letter to expand upon one or two points from your highlights.

PROFILE

Including a profile or summary directly beneath your resume heading is another option. A profile is useful for summarizing a bulk of experience or skills in one particular area or for summarizing the general scope of your career trajectory.

Starting your resume with a profile might be useful in the following situations:

- You have used similar transferable skills in a variety of industries or job functions.

- You have more years of work experience in your profession than you can reasonably fit on your resume.

- You have two or more core areas of expertise that you wish to use together in your next job.

- You have gaps in your work history, or your core experience is not sequential.

An effective profile should be concise and consist of no more than two to three sentences. Don't get overly verbose here—use the same rules of language as for the rest of your resume.

Examples of effective profiles might be:

> "Results-driven marketing professional skilled in establishing brands, creating marketing and public relations strategies, and designing effective marketing collateral. Six years of experience supporting aggressive revenue growth and client acquisition."

> "Fifteen years' experience in architectural engineering and construction project management. Contributed to high-end projects such as

the construction of the new de Young Museum, multi-story residential lofts featuring modern luxury amenities, and refurbishing the central dome of San Francisco's town hall."

"Bringing a Master's degree in cognitive development and extensive studio training in fine arts to the health-care field through clinical art therapy, assisting in cognitive, emotional, and motor skills rehabilitation; board member of the American Art Therapy Association."

When choosing any of these introductions to your resume, select one or two, at most, of those discussed. Never try to fit all three; it will take up too much room, become repetitious, and crowd your resume.

EXPERIENCE

The most important part of any resume, and the section most recruiters will glance at first, is a candidate's experience. For experienced candidates, this section will be created from the past jobs you've held. Entry-level candidates can fill out this section with a combination of work, extracurricular, and volunteer activities.

"" **I'm less inclined to focus on education and more inclined to focus on maturity— what have they done?**

To get started on your experience section, create a master list of your work history in chronological order. List the month and year that you began and ended each job, your job title, the name of the company, and the responsibilities you held. But this is only your preliminary master list to help you see the overall picture of your employment history. Fill out your list by including any particular accomplishments, awards, quantitative results, or recognition you received at each job. After you've mapped out your experience, you'll use your list to select which bits of experience are the most impressive, and to craft your achievement statements for your master resume list.

Seeing your work history laid out chronologically is a good way to identify your progression of roles and tasks, and impress your potential employer with how far you've come in your career. One insider tells us, "I'm less inclined to focus on education and more inclined to focus on maturity—what have they done?" Professional advancement is valued in any field or industry. Your accomplishments build on each other; each skill or responsibility is the foundation for continued growth and the development of expertise. This is true whether you are just starting out or are a seasoned professional.

Achievement Statements

Many people make the mistake of presenting their experience as a simple list of duties held at each job. In most cases, this will not be enough to get a recruiter's attention, especially if you're competing with many other candidates who more than likely hold similar qualifications to your own. Remember that you are trying to sell yourself. Why might a consumer buy one brand of cleaner over another? They both clean, right? But most consumers want the best value for their dollar, and will likely buy the cleaner that they believe will work better, faster, and cost less. These decisions are typically made based on the packaging and marketing messages. The same principle applies to job candidates. Let's say a recruiter is considering several candidates for an account management position. All of the candidates have roughly the same amount of experience, possess mastery over the computer programs necessary to do their jobs, and have maintained budgets. Which candidate will the recruiter call for an interview? The one whom the recruiter believes will work better, faster, and present the most value for the proposed salary.

INSIDER TIP

It is a fact of marketing psychology that odd numbers are more believable and persuasive than even numbers. "19%" sounds like a number lifted off a financial report, while "20%" sounds like a wild guess. Be exact!

It is your job to show in your resume not just the types of experience you've had, but how effectively you performed your duties, what benefits you brought to your employer while working there, and how much more valuable you'll be to your next employer.

Think of your experience in terms of results. Be short on description of duties and long on verifiable outcomes. Quantify your results with numbers wherever possible to give the recruiter a clearer picture of your accomplishments.

Writing Achievement Statements

The format of a cover letter and resume gives you a mere two or three pages in which to express your qualifications. Your job is to make those pages engaging and action-packed. Every word counts. For each bullet point stating what you've done, you'll want to lead with a verb and say in as few carefully chosen words as possible what action was taken, in what setting, with what skills, and with what results. This next exercise will walk you through the process of creating achievement statements that really achieve.

Achievement Statement Example

Environmental Advocate, Sierra Club: Designed and implemented a campaign strategy to educate the public about climate change and shape international treaties on the issue. Generated more than $25,000 in new memberships and donations to support the campaign.

Action: campaigned for environmental organization

Setting: worked with the public

Skills: defined goals, designed campaign, implemented campaign, conducted outreach, educated public

Results: improved public awareness of issues, increased visibility of organization, generated 500 new members ($5,000 revenue), acquired $20,000 in donations

Now it's your turn to try!

WRITE YOUR OWN ACHIEVEMENT STATEMENT

Use this exercise to practice writing your own achievement statements.

Action: _____

Setting: _____

Skills: _____

_____

_____

Results: _____

_____

_____

Situation (job, academic, personal): _____

Statement: _____

_____

_____

_____

_____

_____

EDUCATION

This section might be more aptly titled, "Education and Academic Achievement." Information should include schools attended, degrees conferred, and other data regarding your time in school such as GPA, SAT, GRE, or GMAT scores, scholarships and awards earned, honor society memberships, and class ranking. No need to list high schools attended. Accomplishments in high school generally apply to enrolling in a college, rather than getting a job.

You can also include in this section special certifications, licenses, or additional vocational training you've completed. List only those things that showcase your strengths and are relevant to the job that you're applying to. If your statistics aren't going to wow the reader, you might as well save the space for other, more noteworthy details. Listing *when* you received your degree(s) is optional. Doing so can indicate your age and how current your knowledge is, which may or may not be desirable.

Students with little work experience, particularly those from top-ranked schools, will want to place their education section near the top of their resume, directly beneath the contact information heading, or beneath the objective statement, skills summary, or profile if including any of those.

As your school days grow distant, employers become much more interested in your professional experience than in the fact that you were editor of your school newspaper, or what your major was. Experienced professionals (those a few years or more out of school) should always emphasize work history or experience and save education for last.

Career changers, however, may want to place their education section near the top of their resume if they have little or no experience in the field they wish to enter, but do have education or training in that field.

Selling Your Education

To get maximum mileage out of your education, describe honors, awards, special proj-ects, and coursework. Use the heading "coursework" and you can describe the contents of the curriculum without worrying about the actual *name* of each class. Here's an example:

B.S., Sociology, minor in **Business, 2001**
Michigan State University
Coursework included:

* Financial & Management Accounting
  Corporate Finance
  Statistics and Statistical Analysis
  Principles of Sales Management
  Marketing Strategy & Planning
  Market Research

Computer skills:

* HTML, MS Office, ACT, WordPerfect

Sample research project:

* Discriminant Analysis and Psychographic Profile of Consumer Market for Premixed Ethnic Culinary Ads

---

By fleshing out work you've done in school that is relevant to the job you're applying for, you can skirt around the issue of little work experience or a lack of experience in a particular job or industry, while still presenting yourself as a skilled candidate. If you're leading your resume with your educational accomplishments, you may want to include an objective statement to ensure your that message carries across.

OTHER (ACTIVITIES, ADDITIONAL SKILLS, INTERESTS)

This area is your opportunity to tell the scanner a little more about yourself and add color to your candidacy. If your efforts have been directed to projects outside of work or academia, they will show up here. Details typically include activities, interests, associations, memberships, and skills not already covered, such as proficiency in foreign languages. Such areas of your life may be relevant to how you will perform on the job—and relevance is the key. This section belongs at the bottom of your resume.

WETFEET RESUME TIP

Resume reviewers look favorably on candidates with backgrounds similar to their own. Read the employee profiles included in most firms' recruiting materials and websites and find someone who worked in the same company or attended the same school you did. You'll have a better chance of getting a favorable review.

You can also use the Other section to mention activities that hint at gender, race, religion, or sexual orientation. You may have a slight advantage if your activities indicate that you fall into a group that a particular employer is trying to recruit. This is a touchy subject, but many organizations look to recruit a varied workforce to serve an increasingly diverse clientele. Therefore, highlighting your diversity just might help your candidacy.

Insiders tell us that interesting or unusual information in this section can play a significant role in the decision to award an interview. However, take care in the kind of information you offer. Many people we interviewed say they rejected otherwise decent resumes because of strange mentions in the Other section. For example, saying you won the Twinkie-eating contest at your fraternity by eating 47 Twinkies in 15 minutes isn't necessarily a selling point if you're trying to break into the financial services industry, or most industries for that matter. Also, be sure to avoid any topics that may be controversial.

FINDING YOUR FOCUS

The following table lists the conventional elements that make up a resume so that you can consider them all together. Think of them as pieces of a puzzle; you must decide the best way to arrange them to demonstrate your value to the company or organization. Be sure to check out the sample resumes in the next chapter to get a sense of how these sections work together.

Common Resume Elements

Section	What It Is	Benefits/Drawbacks
Contact Information	Name, mailing address, telephone number(s), email address, website.	Employer can see your current location.
Objective	One-sentence summary of your immediate work goals. Objective section follows the contact information at the top of the resume.	Can be too vague or too obvious, or repeat information in the cover letter. Can help add focus to a resume with varied or little experience.
Summary of Qualifications	Provides the top three or four areas in your background you want the employer to focus on.	Adds focus and highlights strengths.
Profile	Professional summary that captures your focus, skills, and expertise in a few sentences.	Particularly good for professionals with a great deal of experience.
Summary of Skills	Lists most relevant skills/keywords for the targeted position.	Helps reader quickly identify your relevant skill areas.
Education	Degree, major, institution, location, date degree conferred. GPA is optional.	Most employers want to see this information.
Honors/Awards	Academic, scholarship, recognition for contributions in relevant fields.	Demonstrates leadership or academic achievement.

Common Resume Elements, cont'd

Section	What It Is	Benefits/Drawbacks
Certifications, Licensure, Credentials	Important to list if it is a minimum qualification for positions, such as therapists, lifeguards, and engineers.	This information must be current to be useful, especially if licensure is required qualification for position.
Training	Relevant training, continuing education, conference participation.	Shows professional development.
Experience	Can include paid or unpaid positions.	Helpful for those who have little employment history; can include any relevant experience.
Employment History	All relevant employment listed in reverse chronological order (most recent first). Must include date, title, employer, and location.	Employers expect to see this information on all resumes.
Internships	Experiential training you've had as relevant to skills and qualifications.	Most useful to list for new grads or career changers, or if internship is part of academic curriculum.
Activities/ Community Involvement	Volunteer positions, leadership roles, travel abroad, program participation. List dates, titles if any, organization, location.	Shows variety of interests, skills, and accomplishments. Particularly useful if skills are relevant to job.
Language Skills	List only if relevant to the field and you are proficient enough to use your skills on the job. Include level of fluency.	Demonstrates communication competence and multiculturalism.
Technical Skills	Computer programs and lab skills, for example.	Many employers want to see computer competence, even for nontechnical positions.
Research	Includes title, organization, location, project emphasis and outcome, and skills utilized.	Demonstrates specialized knowledge, as well as technical and analytical skills.
Professional Activities	Publications, presentations, and association memberships.	Shows leadership.
Travel	Lists major experiences abroad, dates, and whether travel was through affiliated organizations or independent.	Good for international positions, or to explain time gaps in work history.
Interests	List what you are accomplished at and engaged in.	Gives fuller picture of candidate; controversial interests may not be favorable; takes resume space away from work-related accomplishments.

Packaging Your Presentation

General Formatting Guidelines

Resume Design and Organization

Special Cases

Basic Resume Dos and Don'ts

Mail Merge Morons and Other Big Offenders

Sample Resumes

Why didn't Sam like green eggs and ham? Well, the truth is that he had never tried them. They didn't look very appetizing. Most chefs will tell you that the presentation of a dish, the way it smells and looks, is just as important as the way it tastes. So, now that you've carefully selected and prepared the ingredients of your resume, don't let your dish sit untouched because it doesn't look appetizing. Presentation is the first barrier you'll need to overcome to get that recruiter's attention.

Grab your resume master list—it's time to get down to the nitty gritty and create an actual formatted document. This chapter will tell you what you need to know about arranging and presenting the elements of your resume so that you'll appear as the skilled and competent professional that you are. Those recruiters will be begging for a second helping!

General Formatting Guidelines

Two areas in which you should conform to standard practice in crafting a resume are packaging and content. Resume readers prefer to focus more on content, but it's format that enables them to pick out useful information quickly. To assure a good read, both content and format must be in top shape. As a general rule, the resume is not the place to push the envelope. Remember, resume readers may be reviewing hundreds of resumes for a single position. Few of them will give you extra credit for using bright blue paper or including colorful cartoons. If anything, this will get you snubbed in most fields and for most positions. Good resumes are carefully and deliberately organized and to the point—a quick and informative read.

The format of your resume has one objective: to make your qualifications easy to understand. When formatting your resume, you should adhere to the three Cs—clean, clear, and concise. In business fields, such as financial services or consulting, add a fourth C, conservative. While most resume reviewers don't have a specific model in mind, all seem to appreciate a fifth C, consistency. This generally means:

•   A single, standard font: Times New Roman, Arial, Helvetica, or similar.

•   A readable font size: 11- or 12-point preferred, but no smaller than 10.

•   Neutral paper color: white or off-white.

•   Standard layout: no more than 1-inch, no less than .5-inch margins, left justified, line spaces between sections.

•   One or two pages in length.

•   Aesthetics: white space, symmetry, uniformity.

•   Clear resume organization: a few sections, labeled clearly, chronological listing with dates, and bulleted points.

   HOW LONG IS TOO LONG?

There is no consistent rule as to how short or long your resume should be. Many people believe that resume should exceed one page in length. But most experienced professionals need more space than that to explain their background. Here's a good rule of thumb: Entry-level candidates and those with five or fewer years of experience should try to limit their resumes to one page. Experienced professionals should go no more than two pages. Only curriculum vitaes or resumes for high executives with detailed experience should exceed two pages.

Bullets, which make information easier to scan, are often favored on resumes. Insiders tell us that reviewers are more likely to toss a resume into the "ding" pile than spend extra time plowing through turgid, clunky prose to find what they're looking for. When you make bulleted points, remember to keep them short (one line if possible) and start them with action verbs.

Resist the temptation to use excessive text formatting, graphics, or graphs. Cuteness of any kind may be perceived as unprofessional. Such extras eat up space that could be dedicated to providing evidence of accomplishments and qualifications. Certainly, there are fields where creativity and artistry are appreciated, but it is better to err on the conservative side when you're not certain.

Take a look at the following resume revision. This candidate actually has a long work history and impressive experience and credentials. Look at the original version. What do you gather after scanning the resume for 30 seconds? Not much. But with some prudent editing and formatting, this candidate's excellent work history really shines.

ANYA SAHN   H- (858) 555-9999; C-(858) 555-1010
2300 Lone Ridge Rd.   Email: anyasahn@email.com
San Diego, CA 92126

Objective   To secure a position that my education, knowledge, and skills can be utilized and contribute
              to the benefits of the organization.

Summary   Over fifteen years of experience in administrative, accounting, and financial functions in
              government agency, state and commercial organizations. Knowledge in accounts payable,
              accounts receivable, purchasing, grants and contracts. Graduated with Master of Business
              Administration. Proficiency in MS Office Package – Word, Excel, PowerPoint, and Access.
              Proficiency in operating system such as Windows XP, IFAS, HRIS, including Graphics soft-
              ware. Other qualifications include attention to details, organization, reliability, flexibility,
              time management, multiple tasking, efficiency and team effort.

Experience   AM PHIL Management & Healthcare Services, Inc., San Diego, CA
              Administrator, January 2004 – January 2005
              Overall supervision of RCFE facility including resident care management, human resource
              management, organizational management, and physical environmental management.

              SDCCD – Mesa College, San Diego, CA
              Adjunct Instructor, February 2003 – December 2003
              Taught Business course to college-level students; assessment of students' performance, calcu-
              lation of grades, formulation of evaluation tests, giving lectures, record keeping of student's
              grades and evaluation, and participation in faculty workshops and course development pro-
              grams.

              SDCCD – Miramar College, San Diego, CA
              Accounting Technician, February 1999 – February 2003
              Duties included variety of technical and complex accounting work such as preparation of
              financial statements and reports, analysis of accounting data for submission to the President,
              Vice Presidents and Deans of Schools. Accumulation of accounting data and preparation of
              narrative explanations. Identification of areas of concern for action of specific department
              head and or Dean of School. Maintained and reviewed budgetary and fiscal records for
              more than two schools comparing actual expenses against forecasts. Providing explanations
              of variances as necessary. Monitoring of costs and providing frequent reports to manage-
              ment regarding funds expended and available. Calculation of expenditure projections and
              savings. Communicating accounting changes as necessary to operating units. Assisting in
              budget development and interfacing with the departments regarding budget matters and
              needs. Analysis of situation independently and adopting effective course of action.
              Monitoring, assigning, and verifying, appropriate budget codes, sources, and related infor-
              mation on expenses. Researching and allocation of budget. Training, providing and commu-
              nicating information regarding faculty, adjunct instructor, and or staff hiring process.

Palomar College, San Marcos, CA
Adjunct Instructor, August 2002 - January 2003
Taught an Economics course to college-level students, assessment of students' performance, calculation of students' grades, formulation of evaluation tests, giving lectures, record keeping of student's grades and evaluation, and participation in faculty workshops, and course development programs.

Escondido Union School District, Escondido, CA
Accounting Clerk III, February 1998 – February 1999
Duties included fund accounting, review of capital project costs, management of accounts payables of more than ten vendors, bank reconciliation, and handling of imprest account.

Source Services Corporation, San Diego, CA
Accounting Assistant, July 1997- February 1998
Duties included full cycle, full charge accounts payable functions for more than fifty vendors.

Arnolds Acquisition Corporation, San Diego, CA
Accounts Payable Specialist, February 1996 – June 1997
Duties included full cycle, full charge accounts payable functions for more than ten vendors.

Metro Manila Authority, Philippines
Budget Officer (last held), September 1978 – August 1992
Duties included budget administration, participation in all budgeting phases including preparation, consolidation, review, execution, monitoring and control.   Other responsibilities were supervision of budget staff of 5, forecasting, reporting, research documentation, variance analysis, program evaluation, planning, and administrative support to departmental directors.

Education   Master of Business Administration, National University, 2000-2002
Accounting Program (35 units), Miramar College, 1998
Master of Public Administration (15 Units), MLQU, Philippines, 1983
Bachelor of Arts, University of the East, Philippines, 1977-1981

With some editing, bullet points, and simple formatting, this resume is much easier to quickly scan for information.

ANYA K. SAHN
2300 Lone Ridge Rd., San Diego, CA 92126
858-555-9999 (h) / 858-555-1010 (c) / anyasahn@email.com

SUMMARY
- MBA with more than 15 years of accounting, financial, and administrative experience in government agency, state, and commercial organizations
- Extensive knowledge of accounts payable, accounts receivable, purchasing, grants, and contracts
- Consistent track record of efficiency, attention to detail, organization, reliability, flexibility, and effective resource management

PROFESSIONAL EXPERIENCE

AM PHIL Management & Healthcare Services, Inc., San Diego, CA   01/04–01/06
General Manager
- Oversaw all aspects of 60-patient residential care facility, from bookkeeping and scheduling to maintaining grounds and building.
- Managed staff of 30 administrators and health-care professionals, including hiring, career development, problem resolution, and scheduling.
- Directed vendors responsible for maintaining supplies, facility cleanliness, patient transportation, and repairs.

San Diego Community College District, Mesa College, San Diego, CA   02/99–12/03
Adjunct Instructor, Business Administration (02/03–12/03)
- Taught business course to groups of 20–30 students.
- Developed curriculum, including lectures, reading material, and tests; maintained even split of C- to A-level grades.

Accounting Technician (02/99–02/03)
- Maintained and audited complex budgetary and fiscal records for several schools, comparing actual expenses against forecasts, identifying areas of concern and suggesting solutions.
- Played key role in developing $2.5 million budget, working directly with department to identify available funds and address departmental needs.
- Prepared monthly financial statements and reports and analyzed accounting data for direct submission to the president, vice presidents, and deans of schools.
- Performed quarterly budgetary forecasting, based on monitoring costs, tracking expenses against available funds, and calculating expenditure projections and savings.
- Built data archives and provided narrative explanations of transactions.

Palomar College, San Marcos, CA   08/02–01/03
Adjunct Instructor, Economics
- Taught economics course to groups of 20–30 students.
- Developed curriculum and assessment scale.

Escondido Union School District, Escondido, CA   02/98–02/99
Accounting Clerk III
- Performed detailed fund accounting, reviewed capital project costs, reconciled bank statements, and handled imprest account.
- Managed accounts payable for more than ten vendors.

Source Services Corporation, San Diego, CA   07/97–02/98
Accounting Assistant
- Managed full-cycle, full-charge accounts payable for more than 50 vendors.

Arnolds Acquisition Corporation, San Diego, CA   02/96–06/97
Accounts Payable Specialist
- Managed full-cycle, full-charge accounts payable for vendors.

Metro Manila Authority, Philippines   09/78–08/92
Budget Officer
- Administered $1.2 million budget and participated in all phases of budget development, including preparation, consolidation, review, execution, monitoring, and control.
- Supervised 5-person accounting staff, prioritizing projects, training, providing final review on all financial reports and documents.
- Managed forecast reporting, research documentation, variance analysis, program evaluation, and planning.

EDUCATION
Master of Business Administration, National University, 2002
Accounting Program, Miramar College, 1998
Master of Public Administration, MLQU, Philippines, 1983
Bachelor of Arts, University of the East, Philippines, 1981

COMPUTER SKILLS
Proficient in Microsoft Office and various operating systems such as Windows XP, IFAS, HRIS, and assorted graphics software

Resume Design and Organization

What's the point of choosing all of the right ingredients to include in your resume, if nobody can read it? Clearly, it's not just what's in the resume that counts, but how the information is presented. Typically, the first glance at your resume will last 30 seconds—and in that time the reader will focus on the first third of the page. This means that the information you most want to share needs to lead your resume. Good design and organization will guide the reader's eyes toward the most important sections and points.

The good news is you don't have to go to design school or even take a class to learn the basics of resume design. Understanding the five basic design layouts, which follow, and their relative strengths will give you the information you need to put together a compelling presentation.

 **INSIDER TIP**

Resume readers typically focus on the first third of the page in their initial scan. Make sure your most relevant points are located there.

CHRONOLOGICAL

This layout lists employment in reverse chronological order—that is, the most recent experience is listed first. The convention for many fields, especially business-related fields, this layout best highlights continuity of experience and work history, shows progression in responsibility, and emphasizes titles and employer names.

BASIC CHRONOLOGICAL LAYOUT

Contact info

Experience

Date, title, organization (#1)

• Achievement 1

• Achievement 2

Experience

Date, title, organization (#2)

• Achievement 3

• Achievement 4

Education

Date, degree, school

Additional information

This resume follows a standard chronological layout, emphasizing a long and consistent work history. The summary focuses on the long-term experience and excellent results that make up Lee's professional strengths. The subject specializations function as keywords, quickly informing readers of the applicant's areas of expertise.

LEE JONES
Address
Tel • email

Summary of Qualifications
- Over 14 years tutoring adults and children; serving up to 40 ongoing clients annually
- Develop and teach individualized curriculum based on client abilities and academic goals
- Strong and enthusiastic recommendations from client families and school staff
- Proven results: 99% of students increase their standardized test scores in one or more subjects

SUBJECT SPECIALIZATIONS

- **Standardized Test Preparation**: SAT I & II, SSAT, PSAT, GMAT, GRE
- **Mathematics**: First through twelfth grade – basic arithmetic, pre-algebra, algebra, geometry, trigonometry, pre-calculus
- **English**: Fifth grade through college – spelling, reading, writing
- **Social Sciences**: First grade through college

TUTORING/TEACHING EXPERIENCE

1989-present **Self-employed as Tutor** in high school and junior high school subject areas

2002 **Instructor**, SSAT Preparation Course, Boston, MA
Designed and implemented curriculum for summer intensive SSAT course for private school students.

1989–1996 **Educational Counselor**, Boston Education Service, Boston, MA
Tutored all high school subjects and preparation for SAT with at-risk youth.

1991–1992 **Teacher of English as a Second Language**, International Masters Academy of Britannica, Inc., Tokyo, Japan
Taught English conversation skills to adult students at all proficiency levels.

1989–1991 **Tutor**, A-Level Tutors, Boston, MA
Tutored one-to-one in many subject areas, from university-level Economics to high school English.

EDUCATION

1988 **B.A. in Economics**, Boston University, Boston, MA

FUNCTIONAL

This layout, which organizes your experiences by skill sets or industry areas, is particularly suited for career changers and people with little work experience or who have large gaps in their work history. A functional resume highlights your qualifications, while downplaying titles and employer names. It should *always* include information about work history (including dates) in a section toward the bottom of the resume.

 BASIC FUNCTIONAL LAYOUT

Contact info

Skill/Experience Group #1

- Achievement 1

- Achievement 2

Skill/Experience Group #2

- Achievement 3

- Achievement 4

Work History

- Date, title, organization #1

- Date, title, organization #2

Education

Date, degree, school

This resume follows a functional layout, emphasizing skills and down-playing work history. Take a close look at Leticia's work history—she has held several short-term positions in varied fields and employers (legal service, association, union, and academic institutions). The functional layout is an effective way to emphasize competencies rather than the industries within which a candidate has worked. This style of resume is particularly good for people with little work experience, career changers, and those with gaps in their employment. Note: This style is not typically preferred in conservative arenas.

Leticia Roberts
Address
City, state, zip
Tel
email

SKILLS AND EXPERIENCE

Customer &
Member Services

- Responded to in-coming calls for legal services agency, gave information about the organization, assessed whether caller could be served by the agency, and directed calls or made referrals when appropriate.
- Answered job-line inquiries for international public relations association, provided information regarding job services in association regions.
- Searched association's library files for communication and marketing information requested by members, or referred members to other association resources.
- Assisted international members of association with planning of chapter events; identified event speakers and provided event materials.
- Distributed materials for regional coordinators of study abroad organization, as well as for host families and student prospects. Assisted with processing of host and student applications, coordinated bulk mailings.
- Led small tutorial group for undergraduate political science course; facilitated discussions and advised students regarding term paper topics and writing.

Computer &
Administrative

- Proficiency with Microsoft Office (Word, Powerpoint and Excel) and the Internet
- Maintained financial records for legal services agency and research and education department of international association. Responsible for donor tracking and recognition.
- Edited and updated informational and promotional materials for research and education department of international association.
- Researched text books and compiled annotated bibliography to complement a syllabus for a college introductory course in comparative politics; generated ideas for term projects.

WORK HISTORY

12/01-present	Administrative Assistant; Child Care Law Center, San Francisco, CA
1/00-9/01	Members Assistant; International Association of Business Communicators, San Francisco, CA
11/99-9/00	Office Support Person; ASPECT Foundation, San Francisco, CA
11/98-4/99	Membership Services Officer; National Union of Teachers, United Kingdom
1/98-5/98	Teaching Assistant; Political Science Department, Bryn Mawr College, PA
Summer 1997	Coder; Medical Research Institute, Alcohol Research Group, Berkeley, CA
Summer 1996	Intern; Buck Institute/College of Marin, Kentfield, CA

EDUCATION

2003	Coursework in Asian and Latin American Art History, UC Berkeley Extension

B.A. in Political Science, awarded departmental honors, Bryn Mawr College
Semester program emphasizing art history, Syracuse University in Florence, Italy

COMBINATION

This type of resume includes organizational elements from both the chronological and functional layouts, providing the most flexibility in what you can emphasize. This format works best for job seekers who may want to stick with the more traditional chronological format, but need to emphasize transferable skills, have gaps in their work history, are moving into a new industry, or whose most recent job title was less than impressive.

 COMBINATION LAYOUT 1

Contact info

Skill/Experience Group 1

- Date, title, organization (1st)

- Achievement 1

- Date, title, organization (2nd)

- Achievement 2

Skill/Experience Group 2

- Date, title, organization (3rd)

- Achievement 3

- Achievement 4

Education

Date, degree, school

COMBINATION LAYOUT 2

Contact info

Date, title, organization (1st)

Skill/Experience Group 1

- Achievement 1

- Achievement 2

Skill/Experience Group 2

- Achievement 3

Date, title, organization (2nd)

Skill/Experience Group 3

- Achievement 4

Education

Date, degree, school

This resume combines chronological with functional. This type of layout works well for an individual with a position involving a lot of responsibility, and/or one with a multitude of skill areas. Kurt is an entrepreneur and has experience in every aspect of event planning and management; he organizes his achievements into broad skill areas within his position description. The resume is strong because it emphasizes quantifiable achievements as well as professional awards/recognition.

Kurt Williams, CMP
140 15th Avenue
San Francisco, California 94121
415-555-3434
kw@specialevents.com

SUMMARY
- Extensive experience in coordinating and organizing people, projects, and events
- Highly skilled at developing and implementing program and marketing strategies
- Proven track record of completing multiple projects accurately and within budget
- Certified Meeting Professional

AWARDS
Top 25 Meeting and Event Planners in the Bay Area (Bay Area Business Express, 2002)
Top 15 Meeting and Event Planners in the Bay Area (Bay Area Business Express, 2001)

PROFESSIONAL EXPERIENCE
1998-present   President Special Events, Inc., San Francisco, CA

Event Planning
- Managed meetings with 90-2500 attendees with programs ranging from two to six days
- Developed, managed, and administered program budgets from $60,000-$2.9 million
- Administered budget of $2.9 million, realizing $190,000 surplus
- Collaborated with Program Committee in implementing abstract review and acceptance procedure
- Coordinated speakers' scheduling, hotel arrangements, audio-visual requirements and expense reimbursements
- Managed all on-site operations

Trade Show
- Marketed and managed all logistics of exhibitor trade shows (management of drayage, decoration and security companies, exhibitor contracts and service manuals) with 12-90 vendors
- Inaugurated trade show for bi-annual conference, realizing 25% net profit on $12,500 in sales

Marketing
- Developed promotional programs and execution of collateral materials (logo, marketing announcements, preliminary program, call for abstracts, conference brochure, final program, show directory, conference mementos, convention signage) for conferences of various sizes
- Implemented and supervised direct mailing campaigns
- Wrote and edited marketing copy for product literature
- Analyzed campaign results to monitor effectiveness of marketing execution

Fundraising
- Developed sponsorship packages for bi-annual conference
- Implemented and supervised sponsorship mailing campaigns
- Cold-called targeted sponsor list, realizing $17,500 in donations
- Created first-time live, silent auction, resulting in $14,000 income
- Developed cold-calling process for first-time trade show, selling 14,000 square feet, generating $12,500 in revenue

Personnel Management
- Trained and directed registration team in handling of receipts, confirmations, cancellations
- Trained and managed paid staff and volunteer teams of up to 30 people

1997-1999   **Projects Coordinator** Golden State University, Fairfax, CA

Event Planning
- Coordinated and organized annual weeklong short course exceeding projected attendance by 30%, resulting in 29% increase in net profits
- Managed visiting and distinguished lecturers, including travel, hotel, and dinner arrangements

Kurt Williams, CMP page 2

OTHER EXPERIENCE
1996-1997   **Production Manager** Digital International, Fairfax, CA
1989-1995   **Journeyman Lithographer** Colorgraph, San Francisco, CA
1987-1989   **President** 5 Dimension Printing, San Francisco, CA

PROFESSIONAL AFFILIATIONS
1. Meeting Professionals International
2. Professional Convention Management Association (local chapter Board of Directors)

COMPUTER SKILLS
Macintosh platform: Microsoft Word, Excel, Access, PowerPoint, Outlook, Filemaker Pro, PageMaker, QuarkXPress,
PC platform: Microsoft Word, Excel, Access, PowerPoint, Outlook, Filemaker Pro, Lotus

EDUCATION
1985 B.A., University of California, Irvine

CURRICULUM VITAE (CV)

Used in science and academia, as well as for some international positions, the CV is a formal list of all professional endeavors. There is no limit to the length of a CV. Objective, summaries, travel, and interests are not typically included. CVs used for non-scientific or non-academic positions include personal information such as age, marital status, and nationality.

 BASIC CV LAYOUT, PAGE 1

Contact info

Education

Date, degree, school

Skill/Experience Group 1

•   Date, title, organization (1st)

•   Achievement 1

•   Date, title, organization (2nd)

•   Achievement 2

Skill/Experience Group 2

•   Date, title, organization (3rd)

•   Achievement 3

•   Date, title, organization (4th)

•   Achievement 4

BASIC CV LAYOUT, PAGE 2

Name, Pg 2

Skill/Experience Group 3

• Date, title, organization (2nd)

• Achievement 5

Publications

• Date, title, publisher (1st)

• Date, title, publisher (2nd)

Professional Affiliations

• Date, title, organization (1st)

Honors/Awards

• Date, title, organization (1st)

This sample of a curriculum vitae (CV) is for a doctoral student in the sciences. The CV is most often used in academia, scientific fields, and for executive-level positions. Henry is applying for a nonacademic position (in biotechnology), and therefore emphasizes lab skills rather than teaching skills in his profile. The CV has no limit to length; therefore, Henry has included all relevant professional accomplishments.

Henry A. I. Yee

Dept. of Cellular & Molecular Pharmacology   Phone: 415.555.2345 (H)
Box 0455   415.555.5555 (W)
University of California, San Francisco   email: henryy@cgl.ucsf.edu
San Francisco, CA 94143-0455

Profile

Bio-organic / medicinal chemist with experience in synthetic organic chemistry, biochemistry, and molecular and structural biology
- Designed and synthesized myeloid hormone receptor antagonist
- Identified structural determinants of selective myelomimetics

Education

University of California, San Francisco   1996-Present
  Program in Biological Science (PIBS) – Ph.D. program
  Specialization: Biochemistry and Molecular Biology
  Anticipated Graduation Date: February 2003

University of British Columbia   1991-1995
  B.Sc. Combined Honours Chemistry and Biochemistry

Skills

- Chemistry: Multi-step chemical synthesis, water- and air-sensitive reactions, analytical and prep. HPLC, flash chromatography, ^{1}HNMR and ^{13}CNMR spectroscopy
- Molecular Biology: Transient transfection transactivation assays in mammalian cells, PCR, SDS- PAGE, subcloning and site-directed mutagenesis
- Computer: Irix, Linux and Mac OS X system administration, SYBYL, MidasPlus, Molscript, Raster3D, experienced Macintosh user, some perl and shell scripting and Windows experience

Research Experience

University of California, San Francisco   1997-Present
  Graduate Student
  Research Advisor – Prof. Thomas Smith

Design and Synthesis of Myeloid Hormone Receptor Antagonists
Designed a small molecule myeloid hormone receptor (TR) antagonist by combining the long alkylamide side chain of the estrogen receptor antagonist ICI-164,384 with the myelomimetic GC-1. Prepared several GC-1 analogues with substituents at the carbon atom that bridges the two aromatic rings via 10 to 14 linear step syntheses. Found that HY-4, the analogue bearing the same side chain as ICI-164,384, bound to MR *in vitro* and also behaves as a competitive antagonist in transactivation assays.

Structural Determinants of Selective Myelomimetics
Determined the structural features of the myelomimetic GC-1 that confers its 10-fold preference for binding to the beta isotype of MR in a study comparing GC-1 to 3,5-dimethyl-3'-isopropyl-L-thyronine (L-DIMIT), the non-selective myelomimetic from which GC-1 was designed. Synthesized analogues of GC-1 and DIMIT bearing only one of their two structural differences. Receptor binding and transactivation studies of the analogues demonstrate that the oxyacetic acid side chain of GC-1 is the key determinant for its MRß selectivity.

Publications

- Yee, H.A.I., Maynard, J.W., Boxer, J.D. & Smith, T.S. (2003). Structural determinants of selective myelomimetics. *J. Med. Chem., in Press*
- Yee, H.A.I. & Smith, T.S. (2002). Selective myeloid hormone receptor modulators. *Curr. Top. Med. Chem., in press.*
- Yee, H.A.I., Ng, N.H. & Smith, T.S. (2002). Design and synthesis of nuclear hormone receptor ligands. *Methods Enzymol., in press.*
- Yee, H.A.I., Maynard, J.W., Boxer, J.D. & Smith, T.S. (2001). A designed antagonist of the myeloid hormone receptor. *Bioorganic Med. Chem. Lett.* 111, 3821-3825.
- Smith, T.S., Yee, H.A.I., Ng, N.H. & Castelli, G. (2001). Selective myelomimetics: Tissue selective myeloid hormone analogs. *Curr. Op. Drug. Disc. Devel.* 94, 314-322.
- Castelli, G., Ng, N.H., Yee, H.A.I. & Smith, T.S. (2000). Improved synthesis of the iodine-free myelomimetic GC-1. *Bioorganic Med. Chem. Lett.* 101, 3607-3611.
- Yee, H.A.I, Castelli, G., Mitchison, T.J. & Smith, T.S. (1998). An efficient substitution reaction for the preparation of myeloid hormone analogues. *Bioorganic Med. Chem.* 8, 179-183.
- Castelli, G., Maynard, J.W., Yee, H.A.I., Boxer, J.D., Ribeiro, R.C.J. & Smith, T.S. (1998). A high-affinity subtype-selective agonist ligand for the myeloid hormone receptor. *Chem. Biol.* 59, 399-406.
- Tanaka, S.H., Yee, H.I., Ho, A.W.C., Lau, F.W., Westh, P. & Koga, Y. (1996). Excess partial molar entropies of alkane-mono-ols in aqueous solutions. *Can. J. Chem.* 714, 3313-3321.

Patents

- Smith, T.S., Yee, H.A.I, Castelli, G., & Mitchison, T.J. (2000). Myeloid hormone analogues and methods for their preparation. *U.S. Patent No. 4,220,000.*
- Smith, T.S., Castelli, G., Yee, H., Maynard, J., Boxer, J.D. & Ribeiro, R.C.J. (1999). Selective myeloid hormone analogs. *U.S. Patent No. 5,444,444.*

Special Cases

The classical career trajectory used to mean staying with one company or industry and working from entry-level assistant to associate to partner, or some equivalent sequence of duties and titles. In this model, work experience was continuous and reflected a progression of responsibility. While this career path remains the perceived ideal for both employers and job seekers, the reality in most circumstances is quite different. Today's job seekers often hold positions in a variety of settings, begin their careers after taking time to explore their options, or balance personal goals (like travel or raiseing children) along with their career pursuits. Employers are currently more open to alternatives to the traditional model of professional development than ever before. Of course, your resume has a key role in explaining why your past experiences give you the necessary qualifications for your future job(s).

While recruiters and hiring managers may be impressed with the assets listed in your resume, they will search for potential red flags to probe during the first interview. In particular, they will look for gaps in qualifications or employment inconsistencies, and may even formulate questions directed at resume weaknesses. Read your resume with a critical eye, looking for things that might appear odd or incongruent—for example, position titles that don't seem to correspond to the duties listed or a series of positions that decrease (rather than increase) in responsibility. Be prepared to address these issues should you get an interview.

INTERNATIONAL ASPIRATIONS

Many people hope to work for companies based outside the United States or come from abroad seeking opportunities with American firms. Candidates who may be perfectly qualified for a position could be tossed out of the first stages of the application review process because they are uninformed of the differences that play a role in the international job search.

For the international job seeker, preparing winning job application materials goes beyond researching the position, organization, and industry. Candidates must research the typical hiring practices for the country or regions they are targeting. Most non-U.S. positions require a curriculum vitae, which differs from an American resume (and an academic CV) in its length and in that it includes personal information such as age, marital status, and nationality.

Additionally, international job seekers should be able to point to cross-cultural experiences in their background, as well as specialized and functional expertise (for legal reasons, the employer often must be able to prove that a noncitizen is more qualified than every other candidate in the home country). If you are authorized to work abroad legally, you may wish to include this information in your application materials. Finally, you should have a clear grasp of economics and business practices in the country or region in which you wish to work. So don't be discouraged from pursuing a dream job that's overseas. Just remember that appreciating cultural differences extends to having insight into the expectations of employers in the particular country or region in which you would like to be employed.

LACK OF WORK EXPERIENCE

If you don't have enough experience, expand your definition of experience to include paid, nonpaid, volunteer, community service, political, tutoring, sports, and church/synagogue/mosque/ashram activities. You can even feature classroom experiences if they support your career goal.

Following is an example of a project a student created for a lark. The only pay was a few extra perks around the gym, but look how well it turned out on his resume:

Office of Admissions/Physical Education Department, Fall 1999 and 2000
Orientation Coordinator (Public Relations)

- Conceived role of public relations representative for the Sports Complex in the orientation process; was appointed by the A.D. as "Czar of PR." Won approval for Sports Complex as site of "Bop Tilya Drop" orientation bash.

- Convinced cheerleaders (male and female) to lead Sports Complex tours.

- Increased Sports Complex utilization by over 15% in first year alone. See enclosed letter by A.D. citing my contribution as key to exempting S.C. from budget cuts.

Many students do something for their departments, for a branch of student government, or for a student organization. Sometimes this kind of unstructured "work" can round out the rest of your experience rather nicely.

Here's how one student sold her classroom research as interesting experience to employers:

Sample Projects

- Analyzed all sectors of the Norsk Hydro conglomerate in Norway, including industry and competitive trends, financial management strengths, corporate infrastructure, and historical performance.

- Prepared comprehensive country profile of Brazil's business climate as part of a feasibility analysis of investment and joint-venture potential.

- Developed study of crosscultural organizational behavior investigating corporate communications protocols using Pakistan as a model.

LACK OF INDUSTRY EXPERIENCE

If you suspect that the only people who get interviews are those who have already been in the industry, you're partly right. Certainly, many organizations are biased toward experienced professionals who can "plug in and go." They are relatively safe in assuming that someone who's been in the job before has the skills and characteristics required to do the work. As everyone knows, the best indicator of future performance is past performance. However, employers need to continually bring in new talent as well (the turnover rate is much too high for most organizations to survive on veterans alone). Therefore, if you haven't already developed a track record in the kind of organization, industry, or field you are now pursuing, you should try for the next best thing: demonstrating that you've done the same type of work, albeit in a different context.

How can you do this? As discussed earlier, your resume reviewer will likely be looking for evidence of skills in several areas, such as quantitative and analytical ability, intelligence, drive for results, or teamwork. Think about the things you've done that will showcase your abilities in these areas. Focus on "transferable" skills and experiences you've had that can translate from one industry to another. Additionally, be sure to articulate your career goals clearly and convincingly. Your enthusiasm, willingness to learn, and ability to go the extra mile in your pursuits will make a positive impression on prospective employers.

TIME GAPS

One reason recruiters and hiring managers like chronological resumes is that they want to know whether a candidate took time off between school years or jobs. Be prepared to explain any lapses between jobs or between your sophomore and junior year, for example. If you traveled, have ready an explanation, or anecdotes, that describe something you learned during that time. If you took time off to have a baby or resolve a personal issue, you'll probably need to supply that information to the hiring manager.

It's usually best not to go into a lot of personal detail—insiders tell us this is a warning sign, especially in the cover letter or first interview. But be clear and focus on what you accomplished during that time. Employers want to be sure you can handle intellectual rigor, jobs with increasing responsibility, and balancing your personal and professional pursuits.

JOB HOPPING

If you've been at several companies in just a few years, or never stayed at one company longer than a year or two, you risk being perceived as a job-hopper. Your resume reader may wonder whether you've been fired for poor performance. Frequent career changes sometimes indicate that a person has difficulty sticking with a situation, working through problems, or committing to a job. Many employers look for people who want to stay around for a while—after all, employee turnover is costly in real dollars because of time spent in the search and loss of operational knowledge. However, in today's job market, resume readers are more accustomed to encountering resumes with work histories showing several different employers. If you can clearly articulate how each job has contributed to your professional development and if you can produce strong references, you should have no problem addressing any negative perceptions.

LOCAL YOKELS

If you've spent most of your academic and professional life in Boston, an employer may question your sudden interest in joining the Chicago office of a firm. Consider writing about your goals or perspectives on relocating in your cover letter; this can be addressed with the "why you chose them" paragraph (discussed in the "Writing a Tasty Cover Letter" chapter). Be aware that an employer who is thinking about flying you out for an interview will probably quiz you over the phone before ponying up the funds to pay for you to come out for a face-to-face interview.

PORTFOLIO

The portfolio comprises supporting materials that illustrate the accomplishments you outlined in your resume. Conventionally used by artists (to show samples of their artwork) or educators, the portfolio is becoming valuable to many job applicants, especially those aiming for positions in writing, marketing, advertising, and other creative fields. Your portfolio could contain articles by or about you, writing samples, samples of products you've created (including brochures, printouts of Web pages, business plans, and graphical charts), awards or commendations, school papers or transcripts (for current or recent students). In all likelihood, you won't be asked to submit a portfolio in your job application; however, a portfolio can be a very effective tool during an interview—it illustrates and validates the experiences and skills you want to demonstrate to the prospective employer.

UH OH, WRONG DEGREE!

Let's say you've completed a degree in music history, but now you've decided to pursue a career in financial services. Do you need to go back to school and start all over again? Absolutely not. List your school and the type of degree you received, but omit the major:

> **Stanford University**, Stanford, California
> **Bachelor of Science**, 2000

No matter what your major was, you can feature the coursework that is related to the field you have targeted, as in this example:

> Michigan State University, **Bachelor of Science**, 2001
>
> *Coursework included:*
>
> • Financial & Management Accounting
>   Statistics & Statistical Analysis
>   Research Methodologies for Social Scientists

WETFEET RESUME TIP

Many insiders tell us they develop interview questions according to experience mentioned on a candidate's resume. The best way to prepare for the first interview is to know your resume extremely well. Develop and practice a 20- to 30-second pitch that summarizes your experience and major achievements. You can base this pitch on your objective statements or professional summary/profile. You will use it countless times, to introduce yourself over the phone or in an interview when the interviewer has not had a chance to review your qualifications. Preparing your pitch will help you articulate the items listed on your resume. You should be able to describe points on your resume in a clear, concise, and convincing manner.

Basic Resume Dos and Don'ts

So now you've thoroughly researched your employers, have done some soul-searching, and are on the path toward putting together your perfect resume (or resumes). Here are some dos and don'ts to help you avoid common mistakes while building a stronger, more refined resume (and cover letter).

Do use numbers where appropriate to clearly describe your accomplishments, as in "led a team of nine sales reps."

Don't use vague qualitative terms such as "large" or "many," which leave the reader with questions about specifics.

Do distinguish the important from the trivial in your background to fit the most relevant and significant elements onto a single page or so.

Don't waste resume space with frivolous information, such as "Voted mostly likely to succeed in high school."

Do stick to a basic, clear format that helps the reader glean information quickly and with minimal effort.

Don't try to differentiate yourself with an unconventional format or tactics such as graphics and colored paper, unless you are applying for jobs in arts-related fields.

Do make your resume a document that focuses on your accomplishments and skills.

Don't include reasons for leaving your jobs, salary information, or references on your resume.

Do discuss your two or three most relevant strengths and illustrate them with experience and achievement statements.

Don't try to portray yourself as a jack-of-all-trades in the hope that something will strike the reader's fancy.

Do use the active voice with verbs that indicate you're in charge: "Represented firm at international symposium."

Don't get caught in the passive voice trap, writing as if things happened to you. "Was sent to Argentina to represent the firm . . ."

Do begin each achievement statement with an active verb: "Handled all client correspondence."

Don't refer to yourself as a subject (first or third person) in your resume: "I helped prepare correspondence," or, "Applicant wrote outreach letters to prospective clients."

Do present yourself as a professional, with a straightforward email account and, if applicable, a website that showcases relevant skills and achievements.

Don't include email addresses or websites that have the potential to reveal controversial or inappropriate personal information: Avoid addresses such as sxybb@imacutiepie.com or queenoftheraccoons@hotmail.com.

Do be aware that employers are interested in your eligibility to work legally and may ask for documentation. Take the time to learn about your rights and responsibilities in the workplace.

Don't include personal information such as social security number, age, race, or marital status on your resume (unless you're writing an international CV).

Do use your current home address, a personal email address, and telephone number with a professional outgoing message. Be sure that prospective employers can easily reach you; check your messages regularly.

Don't use your current work email or phone number as contact information. This indicates that you are job searching on your employer's time, something no prospective employer will view positively.

Mail Merge Morons and Other Big Offenders

Remember: When slogging through piles and piles of cover letters and resumes, HR recruiters and hiring managers are just looking for a reason to ding you. If your resume or cover letter fits one of these descriptions, you run a high risk of being shuffled into the "no" pile, no matter how strong your background. So beware!

The Mail Merge Moron

Mail merge morons send their resume and cover letter to Amazon—stating how much they would like to work for Barnes and Noble. As one insider tells us, "If they didn't take the time to even read their cover letter before sending it, how will they be able to produce flawless work once they're here?" Three words: proofread, proofread, proofread!

 INSIDER TIP

Top Five Things Employers Look for When Reviewing a Resume

5. **A well-rounded candidate**

4. **Something that makes you stand out from all the others who are applying for the job**

3. **A balance of work (or academic) and life experiences**

2. **Someone who went to the interviewer's alma mater (not that she's biased)**

1. **A typo—so the employer can throw it out**

High Inflation Rates

Yeah, we know, everyone exaggerates to some extent, but insiders tell us that a resume that looks too good to be true probably is. Therefore, most of them look at a glowing resume with a heavy dose of skepticism. You need to sell yourself and showcase your talents without going overboard. The biggest mistake insiders say that job seekers make is the tendency to overstate experience. "I hate when candidates overstate their actual abilities. Then they get into an interview, and it's a joke. It comes out pretty quickly."

The Title Titillator

Title titillators think a fancy title will make their experience sound better. One insider encountered a resume where a student's employment included being "CEO," Babysitting Service (there were no other employees). Consider the very impressive-sounding title "Director of Strategic Operations." What on earth does that mean? When in doubt, simplify so as to make your role and responsibilities clearer, rather than more obscure. Also, be sure that the title you choose is the one that your former employer or reference will confirm that you had while at their organization.

The Fabricator

Frighteningly enough, many insiders we talked to say they had caught individuals lying about everything from what degrees they had earned to where they had earned them to where they had worked. One remembered a candidate from a top finance school who had lied about being fluent in five languages, one of which was Swedish. It so happened that his first-round interviewer was Swedish. When he began the interview in his native language, the candidate could only blush and admit to lying on his resume. Needless to say, he was not invited back for another interview. Sure, you might not get caught—but why take the risk?

Too Much of a Good Thing

Resumes lacking focus are big losers. They include mentions of membership in seven different clubs without a leadership position in any of them; experience in five industries in the past four years; and knowledge of marketing, sales, manufacturing, finance, and information systems. Right! Avoid looking like a dilettante, and groom your resume so it highlights skills and experiences specifically related to your current goals.

Chek You're Speling

"A typo is death," as one insider puts it. Our insiders say one typo won't disqualify a candidate, but several typos probably will. On the other hand, any typo is a good enough reason to nix a candidate, and depending on the reader's mood and level of patience, a typo might be just the excuse needed to whittle down that pile. Use your spell checker, but be sure to proofread carefully. Spell checkers won't catch all typos and won't check for other hazards such as misused contractions (your vs you're, its vs it's). It's always a good idea to have a friend or two read through your resume before you send it out. Remember, most reviewers are just looking for a reason to throw your resume into the "no" pile.

Technology Hang-Ups

While many recruiters express a preference for receiving application materials by email, don't expect the person on the receiving end to fumble around with an attached file in a desperate quest to review your qualifications. They are much more likely to move right along to the applicants who have sent their materials in a more accessible form. If you have any doubts about the quality of the format in which your resume will arrive, because of platform or application variables, it's best to paste in a text version of your resume in the body of your email. Follow up by sending a hard copy as well to make sure the recruiter gets a look at the formatted version of your resume that you've spent so much time crafting; plus, it shows a little extra initiative, which never hurts. Faxing is almost as fast as email, and often more reliable, although it's definitely a good idea to follow up a faxed resume with a phone call to make sure it was received in legible form.

Sample Resumes

The resumes in this section demonstrate a variety of formats, fields, and professional levels. The examples here are not intended to be copied word for word, but instead should offer you ideas for creating concise statemenst that reflect your strengths. These resumes contain fictionalized names and organizations, but the information is based on real work histories and position listings.

A standard chronological layout is employed to emphasize Jose's activities rather than employment history. This layout works well for someone without a lot of work experience, or whose volunteer and personal endeavors reflect more relevance and responsibility than his or her employment. Jose is currently a student and therefore lists education and related coursework on his resume. Additionally, adding an Objective section helps set the tone for the reader—the information that follows will be viewed in terms of how it supports the objective (in this case, a career in business administration). This format is particularly useful for students and career changers.

Jose Ramirez
jram2@unlv.edu

Permanent Address:
247 Lissom Road
Chicago, IL 30123
(773) 555-1333

Campus Address:
201 Lincoln Ave.
Las Vegas, NV 89154
(702) 444-4444

OBJECTIVE: Summer internship in the field of Business Administration

EDUCATION

UNIVERSITY OF NEVADA, LAS VEGAS (UNLV)   Fall '01 – present
Bachelor of Arts, expected May 2005
Major: Sociology, Minor: Economics, GPA: 3.1
Related Coursework: Microeconomics, Macroeconomics, Probability & Statistics, Statistical Methods in Economics,
Financial Accounting

ACTIVITIES

UNDERGRADUATE BUSINESS SOCIETY, UNLV   Fall '02 – Spring '03
Developed externship opportunities for sophomores and juniors. Contacted professionals in financial and consulting firms and made arrangements for student placements. Updated student members on current events
pertaining to business opportunities and networking; sponsored informational seminars, workshops and speakers.

CENTER FOR VOLUNTEER ACTION, UNLV   Fall '01 – Spring '03
Helped in local non-profit organizations in Las Vegas. Various short-term projects included: tutoring inner-city
kids in multiple subjects, refurbishing dilapidated playground and recreational building, soliciting food donations, and distributing goods to homeless shelters and soup kitchens.

EXPERIENCE

Intern, **CRATE & BARREL**, Chicago, IL   Summer '02
Participated in weekly staff meetings with retail recruiting team, assisted in organizing summer staff orientations
and programs. Created fall schedule for university campus recruiters. Reserved booths at local college job fairs,
and arranged rental car and hotel accommodations for recruiters.

Server, **ROCKET CAFE**, Chicago, IL   Summer '02
Provided friendly customer service in neighborhood restaurant. Worked efficiently as member of team in all
aspects of restaurant operations. Assisted owner/chef in preparing nightly specials, took customer orders,
bussed all tables.

Camp Counselor, **HOOPSTERS BASKETBALL CAMP**, Chicago, IL   Summer '01
Supervised and led activities for youth ages 7-11. Assisted basketball coaches in training and instruction of
children.

COMPUTER SKILLS

Familiar with Microsoft Office, HTML, Javascript and internet search engines

This resume is technically a chronological layout, but works something like a combo resume by emphasizing Marlene's education, professional memberships, and honors and activities, along with aspects of her work experience. The objective statement indicates her short-term goal, as well as a long-term commitment to her chosen career path—a wise move, as many employers hire full-time entry-level employees from their intern pool. Including her availability at the bottom of the resume is also helpful to recruiters who might be planning for the long term as well. Also, Marlene cleverly includes a note about financing her own education through scholarships, showing that she is not only an excellent performer but a self-starter.

Marlene Whitney

m_whitney@email.edu

Current Address:	Permanent Address:
2323 Putnam Road, University, MS 38677	161 Terra Place, Brandon, MS 39047
(662) 555-4444	(601) 555-5555

Objective   To obtain an internship and eventually full-time employment in the field of marketing

Education   **University of Mississippi**, University, MS
Bachelor of Business Administration   Expected May 2007
- Major: **Marketing**; Minor: **Management**
- Major GPA: 3.78/4.00
- *Financed 100% of education with academic scholarships*

Professional   **American Marketing Association**
Membership   Designed and implemented marketing plan for University of Mississippi Speech and
Hearing Center, resulting in a 20% increase in fundraiser attendance

Work Experience *Marketing Assistant and Sales Representative*   Summer 2005
User Friendly, Madison, MS
- Increased product exposure to individual market segments by designing and
  distributing strategic marketing collateral
- Boosted customer walk-in rate with innovative merchandizing, such as compelling
  window and counter displays
- Grew store's customer base through one-on-one interactions with clientele,
  highlighting product features and sales information targeted to each individual
- Facilitated product repair flow, recording detailed information and serving as
  liaison between customers and vendors

Design Assistant   Summer 2002
R. Scott Multimedia and Design, Ridgeland, MS
Improved firm's design productivity by performing detailed preliminary work, such as
importing and formatting graphics and text in various design applications (e.g.,
InDesign, PhotoShop, Illustrator)

Honors &   Sally McDonnell-Barksdale Honors College (August 2003 to December 2005)
Activities   Chancellor's Honor Roll (3.75 GPA or higher), one semester
National Merit Scholar
University of Mississippi Luckyday Merit Scholarship
University of Mississippi Academic Excellence National Merit Scholarship
Boys and Girls Clubs of Oxford (2005)

Availability   Internships: Summer 2006
Permanent employment: May 2007

Trey's resume displays a good synergy between his objective statement, education, skills, and experience. Trey combined academic and work experience under one heading, as the academic work applies directly to his stated objective. His relevant degree and high GPA are emphasized with bolding. Inclusion of Trey's honors and activities shows that there is more to him than just his education.

Trey Arnold Santin

Current Address: Permanent Address:
1780 Alexander Avenue, Apt. 2B   #88 5th Dr., West Mount Road
Washington, D.C. 20009   Champs Fleurs,
(202) 555-2222   Trinidad, W.I.
tasantin@email.com   (868) 555-7777

OBJECTIVE   To obtain a summer internship in the sciences that will allow me to put my theoretical education to practical applications

EDUCATION   **B.S., Chemical Engineering**, expected May 2008
Howard University, Washington, D.C.
GPA: 3.88

SKILLS
- Five years' experience with chemistry laboratory procedures
- Turbo Pascal, C++, HTML, and PeopleSoft
- Familiar with Windows and Macintosh platforms: Word, Excel, and PowerPoint
- Basic written and verbal French

EXPERIENCE   Howard University, Department of Chemical Engineering
Undergraduate Research Assistant, September 2005 to present
- Work directly with professor on fuel cell membrane research
- Carefully document experiments to track and evaluate research progress
- Draw on laboratory knowledge and experience to select apparatus and procedures and perform experiments

Howard University Trio Programs, Washington, D.C.
Tutor-Counselor, Summer 2005
- Improved students' classroom performance through one-on-one tutoring sessions
- Mentored and counseled high school students, improving study skills, focus, and self-esteem
- Coached debate teams to win 1st & 3rd place in Annual Trio Day

Telecommunications Services of Trinidad & Tobago, Belmont, Trinidad, W.I.
Customer Service Representative, August 2003 to June 2004
- Managed approximately 400 customer accounts, preparing invoices, processing service orders, and selling product upgrades

HONORS & ACTIVITIES   Founders' Scholarship, Howard University, 2004 to present
CEACS Alumni Network Scholarship, 2005
National Society of Collegiate Scholars, 2004 to present
Corning Corporate Team Adoption Team Member, 2005 to present
HUSA International Student Liaison, 2005–2006
Conference Planning Chair, NSBE, 2005–2006
Telecommunications Co-Chair, NSBE, 2004–2005
Network Operator, CLDC Lab Howard University, 2004 to present
Church Youth Choir Director, 2001–2004
Sunday School Teacher, 2002–2004
Volunteer, School for Disabled Children, 2001–2003

Lila is currently pursuing her Master's degree in Human Resource Development and looking for a job in human resources after graduation. She lists her education first to emphasize her relevant degree, along with a list of related skills, and membership in two human resources professional associations. Emphasizing these items helps direct Lila's resume toward her chosen career path, since her related work experience so far is limited. But the path is so clear and straightforward that she could even leave off the objective statement to make room for other information that might apply to specific employers.

LILA MACINTOSH

128 Havalin Lane • Philadelphia, PA 19106
215-222-9999 • macintosh@email.com

OBJECTIVE

Seeking a human resources position that will draw on my education, relevant experience, and personal skills

EDUCATION

Philadelphia University   Philadelphia, PA
Candidate: M.S. Human Resource Development (May 2007)
Glennburge University   Buffalo, NY
B.A. Psychology (Cum Laude)

PROFESSIONAL MEMBERSHIPS

- Student member of the Society for Human Resource Management
- Secretary for the Glennburge Chapter of SHRM

RELEVANT EXPERIENCE

American Red Cross, Philadelphia, PA   Fall 2004
Human Resources Assistant
- Managed interview scheduling for candidates and managers
- Performed screening interviews to ensure efficiency in both the recruiting process and use of managers' time
- Represented the organization at "Meet & Greets" to provide information, forms, and applications to candidates
- Assessed employee fit by administering and scoring Predictive Inventory (personality assessment test) and conducting reference checks
- Conducted candidate follow-ups, offering positions and scheduling physicals
- Ensured all employee information was correctly handled and entered into the EEO database

Philadelphia University Human Resource Department   Fall 2004
Graduate Student Assistant
- Helped employees maintain full benefits and pay status by creating and maintaining system to track hours, sick days, and time off
- Determined pension enrollment eligibility by tracking employees' length of service at the University
- Mastered the Human Resource Information System (HRIS) to collect data regarding pension, employee assignments, and accrued sick leave
- Created and disseminated health benefit information packets
- Managed guest list for annual employee recognition ceremony
- Triaged all incoming queries to manage call volume and provide efficient customer service

SKILLS

- Microsoft Office: Word, Excel, Power Point, Outlook, and Access
- HRIS, SPSS (Statistical Package for the Social Sciences), ABStat (statistical software), and Dreamweaver

Michael's resume is a great example of the simple, straightforward approach. He is looking to start a career in accounting but has no past work experience in that field. In the top third of his resume, Michael highlights his accounting degree, professional development course, relevant computer skills, and language skills to make his case. The work experience is kept brief and occupies the bottom half of the resume, deemphasizing it.

MICHAEL CHING

1735-B Lamont Street
Brooklyn, New York 11206
(718) 333-2222; (212) 444-6666
m_ching17@email.com

Objective	Seeking a challenging entry-level position in accounting support
Education	Bachelor of Science, Accounting, expected May 2006 City College of New York, New York, NY
Professional Development	Microsoft Office Specialist Expert Certification (pending)
Computer Skills	Quicken, QuickBooks, Microsoft Word, Excel, PowerPoint, Internet research
Language Skills	Bilingual English/Chinese (Cantonese and Mandarin)

Work Experience   *Teaching Assistant (contract)*   3/05–5/05
New York Chinese Baptist Church, New York, NY
- Instructed bilingual students one-on-one in practical computer applications and use of the Web
- Perfected interpersonal communication skills by helping non-native speakers improve English language use and understand U.S. culture

Sales Representative (contract)   5/05–8/05
Vector Marketing, Inc., Flushing, NY
- Improved professional relationship building and communication skills by conducting public product demonstrations

Counter Server   1/02–6/02
Ambiente Consecutivo, Inc., Louisville, KY
- Assisted in detailed inventory process, tracking supplies and forecasting ordering needs
- Served customers directly in a high-touch, fast-paced environment; consistently lauded for maintaining excellent customer relations

Here's an example of a functional layout, with skills emphasized and work history downplayed. Bettina is an accomplished lawyer, but is changing careers to that of program manager/administrator. She targets three top skills she believes (based on careful research!) characterize program management. In addition to promoting her skills, this resume reflects the industry/fields with which she has expertise (disability rights and education).

BETTINA RAY MUELLER

45 Lakeshore Drive
Richmond, CA 94804
(510) 555-2773
bamueller@worldnet.att.net

OBJECTIVE: Apply my distinct qualifications learned as an attorney to the field of program administration.

QUALIFICATIONS

Organizational skills
- Coordinated day-to-day activity in 20 class action cases involving physical access to public accommodations
- Organized litigation project concerning physical and programmatic access in California schools
- Managed intake system for nonprofit law firm receiving more than 5000 calls a year
- Updated and maintained computer database of 100+ children's advocates

Communication skills
- Counseled and represented families in educational matters
- Resolved families' legal educational concerns through communication with school district personnel and counsel, social workers, and probation officers
- Conducted workshops for community, professional, and parent groups
- Conducted interviews and deposition preparation with clients

Research and writing skills
- Drafted comments to proposed amendments to federal Individuals with Disabilities in Education Act
- Wrote federal and state memoranda of law, pleadings, and discovery
- Analyzed and summarized voluminous production documents
- Conducted legal research in substantive areas of education, disability, employment, and civil rights law

EMPLOYMENT

Education Law Center, Intake Attorney, Philadelphia, PA	6/01-6/02
Disability Law Project, Attorney (contract), Philadelphia, PA	3/01-5/01
Honeywell & Associates, Attorney, Philadelphia, PA	9/00-3/01
Disability Rights Advocates, Attorney, Oakland, CA	2/99-6/00

EDUCATION

Golden Gate University School of Law, Juris Doctor, San Francisco, CA, May 1999

Claremont Pitzer College, Bachelor of Arts, Anthroplogy/History, Claremont, CA, May 1995

Elizabeth's straightforward job history speaks for itself. The path from her relevant education to internship to full-time position sets up the logical next step in her career. So Elizabeth uses the primary section of her resume to explain her numerous job responsibilities. She has broken down her achievement statements by area, making it much easier for a recruiter to scan her detailed accomplishments. Including her experience abroad, award and honors, and other activities shows that she is a well-rounded candidate, a desirable trait among many employers.

ELIZABETH TACHINAU

16-B Pearl Creek Road, Evanston, IL 60201
(314) 555-6666 tachinau@email.com

Experience

Midwest Investment Group, LLC, Chicago, IL   June 2004–present
Global Operations Associate, Reconciliation and Control Group

   Stock Loan: Balance and settle stock loan borrows and returns for 8 international and 7 domestic accounts daily. Requires close attention to detail to identify costly breaks, strong communication skills in speaking to traders and account reps, and vast knowledge of stock loan product, laws, and general practices in various countries.

   - Improved error identification process by creating a system for compiling, sorting, and distributing all international stock loan instructions, resulting in faster problem resolution and freeing up traders' time.
   - Streamlined training process by creating guidelines and cheat sheets to shorten learning curve; trained and mentored 3 co-workers on daily stock loan procedures.

   Billing: Audit 8 international and 7 domestic month-end prime broker bills for stock loan fees/rebates totaling $15–20 million per month.

   - Developed new process that consolidates all daily stock loan breaks, allowing easier identification of monthly issues to enable company to request specific and relevant refunds.
   - Researched and compiled all billing processes to clarify fees being paid and determine additional resources needed.

   Prime Broker Accounts: Balance cash of 5 prime broker accounts daily. Identify discrepancies that arise from trades, financing charges, corporate actions, and dividends. Route issues to correct groups, account reps, or traders. Reconcile trade positions accounts in a timely manner so that traders can confidently trade on accurate positions.

   Futures: Balance cash and positions in same manner as prime broker accounts but on more challenging futures product, requiring an understanding of open trade equity and commission discrepancy issues specific to futures.

Global Finance, Inc., Chicago, IL   January 2004–March 2004
Internship, Asset Management

   - Designed a critical orientation and training program for new hires in the Chicago Asset Management group.
   - Integrated training requirements of all teams, including client service analysts, internal wholesalers, operations, distribution services, financial control, business analysis, and compliance.
   - Collaborated and consulted with middle- and upper-level managers of various divisions to develop a successful training program. Presented final product upon project completion.
   - Generated hypothetical mutual fund performance presentations and Morningstar X-Ray literature for internal wholesalers.

Education

   Northwestern University, Evanston, IL   June 2005
   Bachelor of Arts in Economics; minor in Spanish. Cumulative GPA: 3.70/4.00

   Universidad Panamericana, Mexico City, Mexico   Summer 2003
   Summer study-abroad program with research concentration on Mexico's economic and political status. Produced 20-page research paper examining the effects of NAFTA on Mexico.

Awards and Honors

   Invited to participate in Economics Honors Program
   All-Alpha Kappa Psi Academic Team, 2003–2004

Activities

   Career Peer, Northwestern University Career Services: Advised and educated peers on career-related issues, presented career information to groups as large as 240 people.
   Peer Advisor: Directly supervised and assisted groups of incoming freshmen.
   Alpha Kappa Psi Professional Business Fraternity
   Alpha Chi Omega Sorority

Tiana has amassed more than five years of experience in her career and has followed a linear career path with clear advances in responsibility and professional status. More than one page is necessary to lay out her advancement and numerous professional accomplishments. Tiana includes a brief description of each employer, adding further specificity to her achievements. This is particularly important to this career path, as specific industry experience is important in public relations. Presenting her linear work history in this way, Tiana is clearly prepared for the next step in her career.

Tiana Rosa deLossi
3917 Powell Street #320 San Francisco 94115
415-555-3333   tianadelossi@email.com

EMPLOYMENT HISTORY

PR Account Manager, Rogue & Partners, San Francisco, CA   06/03 to present
Rogue & Partners is a lifestyle PR agency serving a wide range of internationally renowned brands, including **Diamond Hotels**, **Seasonale**, and **Astronica Wine Group**.
- Develop innovative campaign strategies by identifying message points, key media outreach, pitch points, and timelines
- Secure high-profile client coverage through local, national, and international media outreach; have landed exposure on two nationally syndicated talk shows, local news channels, and numerous national magazines
- Organize and host high-attendance media launch parties, managing all event logistics and promotion
- Maintain relations with account base through monthly reports and presentations and secure new accounts by leveraging existing contact relationships; have secured 5 key accounts
- Craft media documents, including press releases and press packs, strategically targeting client brands to specific markets

Publicity & Marketing Manager, Hot Iron Press, San Francisco, CA   11/01–06/03
Hot Iron Press publishes award-winning illustrated lifestyle books that specialize in food, interior design, and gardening titles.
- Managed national publicity campaigns from concept to completion for major title releases
- Coordinated author tours, successfully booking high-profile national and local media coverage
- Designed creative mailing packets and press information for national dissemination
- Developed key new relationships with national lifestyle press and broadcast media through networking; built reputation though recognition for successful campaigns
- Maintained campaign efficiency and innovation by managing freelance publicists and designers

Marketing & PR Officer, Raza Communications Publishing, San Francisco, CA   08/00–11/01
Raza is one of the world's largest publishers of television and film publications. The portfolio of titles includes the official magazines and books for many of the leading entertainment brands in the U.S.
- Successfully designed and implemented global corporate PR and marketing strategies using print and online media
- Developed and managed key international relationships with major media producers
- Performed market analysis and developed future publicity strategies with company directors

PR Assistant, Extreme Motors, San Rafael, CA   04/00–08/00 (contract)
During my time with the company, I gained extensive experience interacting with all sectors of the media from a political, environmental, and lifestyle perspective. I also developed a better understanding of international public affairs and the corporate culture of an international business.
- Assisted in developing an emerging strategy to enhance company image
- Helped release product information to the press, coordinate major events, and create marketing collateral

Managing Editor, Auto Media Inc, San Rafael, CA   06/99–04/01
Under my management, Auto Media became California's definitive automotive news and information source.
- Promoted to Managing Editor after only 3 months as Marketing Executive
- Increased readership by 500% per month
- Developed a 5-year business plan, aiding business development and revenue generation
- Designed a European launch strategy
- Created, commissioned, and managed site content and marketing material
- Wrote/researched news stories and live reports from national events

EDUCATION
Coventry University, BA, Media, Culture & Communication (Honours)   09/95–07/99
- Internship, Marie Claire, IPC Magazines, London
- Publishing Program Certificate from U.C. Extension

AWARDS & MEMBERSHIP
- Awarded travel fellowship for outstanding research into cultural geography of Los Angeles and San Francisco
- Committee program member of the Northern California Book Publicity and Marketing Association

COMPUTER SKILLS

Photoshop	Microsoft Word	Microsoft Access	Bacons Media Source
QuarkXPress	Basic HTML	Microsoft Excel	Factiva/Nexis Lexis

Writing a Tasty Cover Letter

Pique Their Appetite

General Cover Letter Guidelines

The Ingredients of Your Cover Letter

Cover Letter Dos and Don'ts

Email Cover Letters

Sample Cover Letters

Pique Their Appetite

By now, you should know what ingredients make up an appealing job application. If you are going to prepare an irresistible entrée, you'll need to have an understanding of the employers' "taste" in employees—qualifications, skills, and fit with the corporate culture—and you'll need to know what's in your pantry—the achievements and skills available to you for seasoning your application. But if you are to get any employer to try out your main course, your resume, you first need to pique their appetite with a tasty appetizer: your cover letter.

Like a good appetizer, all cover letters have one main purpose: to whet the reader's appetite, get them interested enough to move on to your resume and then want to interview you. In many cases, the cover letter is the first thing the employer encounters about you, so make this first impression a good one. If the letter doesn't have a hook that makes the reader curious to know more, your resume won't get a glance.

A cover letter should always be included with your resume, whether you're prospecting a potential employer that you have no previous exposure to or pursuing a personal recommendation. The cover letter shows that you've spent some time and thought on your application as well as gives you the opportunity to present a bit of your personality, and hopefully, stand out among other candidates. It should also show that you have a direct and specific purpose in contacting this person—that you know who you are and what you can offer them.

That said, some employers confess that they don't read cover letters. Other employers pay no attention to cover letters unless they notice a problem (poor writing, grammar mistakes, too generic, too long). So, while the lack of a cover letter or a poorly written cover letter can definitely hurt you, a well written cover letter never will. And in some cases, it may be your only ticket to the interviewing room. So, how do you write the thing?

There is often a lot of confusion surrounding cover letters. Why should you include them? What makes a good one? How long should it be? What should it say? The first thing to keep in mind is that, like your resume, the cover letter is not just a utilitarian device explaining why you are contacting a potential employer—it is a marketing piece. And, like any good marketing piece, it should grab your audience's attention and sell them on the value of your product—you. The cover letter is the first piece of your marketing package, and should hook the reader into examining your resume. And, like it or not, this requires some skill and savvy.

General Cover Letter Guidelines

In cooking, basic ingredients form the start of a good dish, but the way you combine the ingredients also affects the outcome. The same is true for your cover letter. Careful choice of words, tone, and aesthetics are essential to creating a pleasing product.

The "Write" Stuff

Insiders tell us that cover letters are used to assess an applicant's ability to write clearly and concisely. For example, candidates with a strong technical focus and international candidates whose first language is not English undergo this type of scrutiny when seeking a position in the United States. As with your resume, be sure to proofread for typos.

Lookin' Good

To increase the professional look of your application, use the same paper, contact information, header, and font style in both your cover letter and resume. It is acceptable (and often encouraged) to email applications. For more on this, see the "Contacting the Employer" chapter later in this guide.

A Well-Tuned Tone

The tone of your cover letter in most circumstances will be professional but thoughtful, persuasive but restrained. Use concise sentences and be direct. At the same time, be sure to inject plenty of enthusiasm and genuine interest into your letter.

Custom Content

In your cover letter, include information that truly tailors the application to a particular employer and specific job opening. Complement and reinforce the qualifications presented in your resume, using words and phrases from the employer's job listing and/or website.

Here are some points about content you'll want to keep in mind as you write your letter:

1. How you learned of the job or company is important to recruiters and hiring managers, especially if there is a mutual connection that can speak of your qualifications.

2. Demonstrate a good fit with the employer's corporate or organizational culture. Be sure to back up any assertions of personal characteristics by describing the resulting achievement either on your resume or in your cover letter. Ideally, the cover letter refers to information found on your resume without being repetitive or redundant.

3. Go beyond the resume in explaining your situation and career direction. For example: "My career goals include gaining leadership experience in the delivery of financial advising services and working in a private business setting that supports high-quality customer care. I will be able to relocate for this kind of opportunity."

4. Avoid discussing weaknesses or making excuses; instead, explain your situation in a way that indicates a sense of purpose and that you've learned something of value from your experiences. For example, if you've been laid off, what have you done to be productive since losing the job (e.g. volunteering your time for a worthy cause, reaffirming or reshaping your career goals)?

5. If salary requirements are requested in a job posting, discuss them in your cover letter. It's best not to trap yourself by naming a specific amount. Instead, say something like "my salary requirements are in step with the responsibilities of the position and the expertise I would offer your company."

The Ingredients of Your Cover Letter

There are two basic types of cover letters: Those developed to respond to a specific job opening and those that serve as letters of introduction. The latter is sometimes called a broadcast letter, and it can function like a "cold call" to develop opportunities where no immediate job opening exists.

While your cover letters should follow a basic structure, it's best to avoid creating a form letter. Your goal is to entice employers with a clear, concise, and well thought-out summary that suggests that you offer exactly what they need.

THE BASIC COVER LETTER FORMAT

Fortunately, when it comes to cover letters, there is a general recipe to follow. Once you learn it, you'll be able to vary your approach to suit each position, industry, and employer preferences.

Every cover letter should include:

- Your contact information

- Date

- Employer's contact information

- Paragraph 1—introduction (why you are writing)

- Paragraph 2—what you offer them

- Paragraph 3—what happens next

- Closing

This structure contains all of the information you'll need to tempt a recruiter to review your resume, whether you're applying to a specific opening or initiating contact with a firm that is not advertising opportunities. The basic structure of the cover letter provides a frame upon which you can build to conform as closely as possible to the requirements and preferences of your targeted employer.

Avoid "canned" letters! Recruiters and hiring managers tell us that formulaic letters often end up in the discard pile. The applicant who customizes his or her words is more appealing, and will be given preference over others. One insider puts it this way: "The cover letter is the one opportunity they have to talk to me." Employers don't want to waste their time on a candidate who is not genuinely interested in the position and their company.

 INSIDER TIP

Top Five Things Recruiters Look for in a Cover Letter

5. **"Readability"**

4. **A sense of the applicant's personality**

3. **How an applicant found out about the job opening**

2. **Something eye-catching such as a major accomplishment**

1. **Evidence that the applicant has researched the company**

THE FIRST BITE: WRITING AN EFFECTIVE INTRODUCTION

"It was the best of times, it was the worst of times . . ." is one of the most famous first lines in history. Imagine if Charles Dickens had begun *A Tale of Two Cities* with something like, "I write novels and this story is about England in the 18th century. . ." The book wouldn't be nearly as famous—because most readers would not have got past the first line. Although you're not crafting the Great American Novel here, you are trying to do something like what Dickens did: grab your reader's attention with the very first line—and hold on to it.

This may sound like an impossible feat, but if you have done your research on the companies you are applying to, and are applying to them for the right reasons, this shouldn't be that hard. For example, to job hunt in the most effective way, you should be applying to the companies where you have the best chances—those which you have some connection to through a contact, experience, particular interest, or the like.

INSIDER TIP

Avoid "canned" letters! Recruiters and hiring managers tell us that formulaic letters often end up in the discard pile. The applicant who customizes his or her words is more appealing, and will be given preference over others.

Your introduction will be the most customized part of each cover letter you write (and yes, you will be writing a unique cover letter for every job for which you apply). A good way to start thinking about your introduction is to catalogue the things that draw you to a particular job in the first place. What's the standout feature that will distinguish you from other applicants? Did a mutual friend or colleague tell you about the opening? Are your skills so well suited to the job that the description practically restates your resume? Have you and your family been using the company's products for years? Were you a volunteer in the Peace Corps just like the hiring manager was? These are the kinds of things that will pop out to a hiring manager—and will differentiate and personalize your application.

After you've listed some of your connections or attractions to the job, draft a few openers to see which connection will be the most effective. Does it have to be a work of art? No. The key is to have a particular reason for contacting the company. This is why generic broadcast letters generally raise the ire of most hiring managers. If you're just sending them the same letter that you've sent to hundreds of other companies and haven't taken the time to really find out about their company or the job opening, why should they take the time to read your application? Don't waste your own time or a potential employer's by using a boring, generic introduction.

SATISFY THEIR CRAVING: STATE WHAT YOU OFFER

After you've caught your potential employer's attention with your opener, it's time to tell them why you're contacting them and what you have to offer. Let's repeat that: what *you* have to offer. It is *your* job to sell yourself to the employer. And that means showing them something you have to offer that will benefit them. You should know what that is from the research you've done on the employer and the job opening.

Think of your letter in terms of the reader's interest. Put yourself in the employer's shoes. What would you be looking for? What would get you interested in a candidate? What are the most important qualities in a candidate for this position? What about your company's culture would make a particular candidate attractive?

This might be specific skills, talents, experience, or contacts in a field. Don't be tempted to fill in this section by restating bullet points from your resume. That would be redundant and a waste of the recruiter's time. Craft a few compelling, overarching statements describing your fit with the job that will help the reader quickly assess what you have to offer. These statements should be designed to persuade the reader to look at your resume and find out more about you.

You might summarize your years of experience in a trade: "I bring 10 years of experience in the consumer products industry," or "My combination of marketing and management skills should be just what you need," or "This job represents the perfect amalgamation of my education and experience in art history and my practical marketing skills." Summarize and entice, but don't repeat your resume.

Now go back to thelist of achievement statements you created for your resume. Next to that, list the particular needs of your potential employer based on the job listing or your research. By comparing these two lists, you should be able to prioritize the employer's needs and match those to your fine qualities.

Once you've chosen your highlights, rewrite them into an effective paragraph that follows your introduction in a way that makes sense. For example, you and the recruiter are both tennis enthusiasts and you've mentioned that in your opener. Go on to point out how your love of tennis is based on a sense of friendly competition and precision, which are the same qualities you've learned from your years as a [fill in the job title].

A SATISFYING FINISH: INITIATING THE NEXT MOVE

Now that you've grabbed the recruiter's attention and got her interested in your qualifications, don't just leave her hanging. Take charge and state what the next step will be. These statements should be assertive, but not overly aggressive. Keep in mind that you're a professional engaging in business communication to establish a mutually beneficial relationship. Your final paragraph can state your intention to contact the employer to set up an interview, create a sense of urgency to compel the employer to contact you, present an offer that the employer cannot refuse, or any other irresistible tidbit that you come up with.

 INSIDER TIP

In fields such as investment banking or consulting, a bull market is taken for granted until there's a problem. This can also be true when job searching and submitting cover letters through an on-campus recruiting process. Where this may be the case, we recommend a low-risk strategy. The cover letter should be kept short and to the point, with a maximum length of a half page. Be sure to include all of your critical information in your resume, because there's a good chance your cover letter won't be read.

SOME STRUCTURE TO GET YOU STARTED

 COVER LETTER FORMAT

The following is a general outline that you can use to create your own cover letters.

Your Header

Address, telephone, e-mail

Date

Employer Name
Title
Org
Address

Dear _____,

I am writing to submit my application for a _____ position in your _____ [city, state or location] office. I am currently a _____ at _____, and it is with enthusiasm that I ask to contribute my training and experience to this new position.

I have been a _____ working on _____ for nearly _____ years, and I am committed to pursuing a career in _____. While I have greatly enjoyed and appreciated the opportunity to work at the forefront of these issues while at _____, I feel the need for a personal and professional change. Your organization is poised to _____, and it is truly exciting to see the _____ in your [city-location] office. This position offers the opportunity to participate in _____ _____.

COVER LETTER FORMAT

I believe that my work experience makes me well suited to assume the responsibilities of a _____ position. [Give examples.]

As you can see from my resume, my background in _____ extends beyond my work history at _____. As a result of my experiences, I have become a quick learner who _____. [Describe more skills and personal qualities that match the position.]

I would welcome the chance to discuss this opportunity with you at your convenience. If you have any questions or require any additional information, please do not hesitate to contact me via e-mail at _____ or by telephone, ___-___-____. Thank you very much for your time and consideration. I look forward to hearing from you.

Sincerely,

Your name

_____

Enclosure: Resume

This cover letter outline is geared toward responding to a particular position opening. The format could easily be converted to a broadcast letter by changing the first paragraph to:

I am interested in pursuing career opportunities in your _____ [city, state or location] office. I am currently a _____ at _____, and it is with enthusiasm that I ask to contribute my training and experience to your organization.

Cover Letter Dos and Don'ts

As you start writing your powerful, compelling cover letter that will entice any employer to take a good long look at your equally powerful resume, keep these basic principles in mind:

Do address your cover letter to the proper hiring manager, by name. Don't know who that is? Do some research, or pick up the phone and call. Still can't find out who the correct person is? Then address your letter to the name of the human resources manager who will probably be reading the letter.

Don't misspell anyone's name, confuse their job title or department, or incorrectly name the job you're applying for. Pay close attention to the language used in the job listing, if you're responding to one, and double-check any personal names you use.

Do craft a compelling opening line that will draw the reader into the body of your letter.

Don't try to be too cute or use humor that might not be funny or appropriate to everyone.

Do point out any connections you have to the company, either through a colleague, background in the company's business, or particular interest in the company's service or product.

Don't restate the facts of your resume. Your cover letter should complement your resume by introducing you in a personal way, stating your reasons for applying for a particular position, and enticing the hiring manager to look at your resume next. You might expand on special projects or skills listed in your summary, but don't include what can easily be read on the resume.

Do craft clear, concise sentences that are error-free and professional, without being stuffy or fluffy.

Don't go on and on and on. You should be able to state your case in three to four well-crafted paragraphs.

Do be convincing and assertive with your letter. You don't want to come off as passive.

Don't be arrogant or presumptuous. You are the one approaching the employer, after all.

Do state the next step, as in "I'll call to set up an appointment," "I am available on Tuesday afternoon for an interview," or "I'll follow up next week to answer any questions you have."

Don't use bloated or flowery language. Make your statements clearly and get to the point as quickly as possible.

Do include all of your contact information in your cover letter. There is always the chance that your resume and cover letter could be separated, and you don't want to leave a potentially interested hiring manager with no way of contacting you.

Don't rush through writing your cover letter. As we stated before, while cover letters are not always read, a poorly written one will send your application to the "no" pile as quickly as a poorly written resume will.

Do show a bit of your personality. You're trying to get the hiring manager to like you and want to meet you.

Email Cover Letters

These days, many job seekers send their job applications via email. While this can certainly make a job search proceed more efficiently (and indeed, many employers prefer this method, as resumes are often stored in electronic databases), pitfalls in sending electronic correspondence to a potential employer are common and all too easy to stumble into.

You should always include a cover letter with an emailed resume, just as if you were sending a hard copy. The cover letter is the body of your email, which explains why you are contacting the employer and serves the exact same purpose as a traditional cover letter—to compel an employer to scroll down and read or open your attached resume.

LENGTH

An email cover letter should be shorter concise than a traditional hard-copy cover letter, and should follow certain technical specifications. An emailed cover letter should be no more than two to three paragraphs—under 150 words, ideally—and should not exceed one screen length.

An email cover letter is perhaps even more important than a traditional hard-copy letter accompanying a resume, because a recruiter will actually have to make the decision to click through and open an attachment, rather than just flipping to and scanning a second page of a hard-copy package. Getting to the point quickly and convincing the recruiter that your resume is worth a look is crucial—and you have less time and space in which to do that in an email environment.

Your email cover letter should quickly lay out your reasons for contacting the employer and summarize your key qualifications.

Don't go into unnecessary detail about your accomplishments or wax poetic about what a great company the recruiter represents. You're simply giving the recruiter enough information to determine whether your resume is worth a look. An indirect, lengthy email cover letter will quickly be deleted.

THE SUBJECT LINE

Email subject lines present a unique opportunity—or a unique hurdle, depending on how you look at it. While a recruiter scanning through a stack of hard-copy cover letters and resumes essentially has to scan your letter to determine what you want, a recruiter scanning emails in an inbox could choose to skip your letter altogether if the subject line is absent or not compelling. Or he could choose to pass over the other candidates and go straight to your letter if the subject line gives him what he's looking for.

The subject line should be as specific as possible, without being too lengthy. Something like "Web developer w/ 5 yrs' experience" or "Government policy legal clerk" will be much more effective than a job number or—gasp!—no subject at all. Read application instructions carefully to see if a job number or specific use of the subject line is required.

KEYWORDS

An email job application represents a great opportunity to include keywords, as many applications and resumes will be stored in a database and retrieved later through a search. Wherever possible, include keywords directly from the job listing or employer's website in your email cover letter.

FORMAT

Always use plain text (ASCII text) when sending an email cover letter. Not all email programs can interpret style choices such as fancy fonts, italics, boldface, or bullet points. To play it safe, stick to black Arial 10-pt font with a white background. Use dashes, asterisks, or capital letters for emphasis—but be sparing.

The easiest way to make sure your email cover letter text is stripped of any fancy formatting is to compose it in a Word document, then save it as a plain text document. Any text styling will automatically be eliminated once it is saved in a text-only format.

When pasting your message into the body of your email, make sure the line length is no more than 60 characters. Some email programs may have smaller viewing windows, which will fragment your message and display it on multiple lines of varying lengths.

Some word processing programs will allow you to set your margins to a desired width—60 characters—and then save as "text only with line breaks." This will ensure that your message arrives in its original form with spacing intact. If your word processing program doesn't allow you to save a document as "text only with line breaks" (some don't), then simply break each line by hand once you've pasted your message into the email body by inserting a paragraph return at 60 characters or less.

PASTE IN YOUR RESUME

You should always include your resume in the body of your email, whether or not you are including it as an attachment. Many recruiters may not want to take the time to open an attached resume, or they may avoid it to due to fear of viruses. Many companies don't even accept emails containing attachments, so a quick call to the company to check on this will ensure that your message is properly received. Your text resume should follow the same guidelines as your cover letter, using plain text format and line lengths of no more than 60 characters.

Sample Cover Letters

The letters in this section demonstrate a variety of formats, fields, and professional levels. Don't take the examples here as prescriptions. Instead, use them as inspiration for creating concise correspondence that reflects your strengths. These letters contain fictionalized names and organizations, but the information is based on real work histories and position listings.

A SPECIFIC POSITION

Although somewhat lengthy, this letter does a thorough job of emphasizing the relevant skills and goals of the applicant. Note that it is addressed to Human Resources and therefore includes the job number as a subject header. Ideally, addressing an individual is preferable to just going with "Human Resources Administrator"; you can call the organization to inquire about the hiring person's name and title.

LETICIA ROBERTS
Address
City, state, zip
Telephone
Email

June 10, 2003

World Art Museum
200 Lafayette Street
San Francisco, CA 94100
FAX: 415-555-9410

RE: Position # 436654, Membership Assistant

Dear Human Resources Administrator:

I am applying for the position of Membership Assistant with the World Art Museum. I learned of the opportunity through your online posting on Craigslist.org, and feel that my qualifications are a good match for the responsibilities of the position.

I have several years of customer service and administrative experience in the nonprofit community. As Member Services Assistant for the International Association of Business Communicators (IABC), I responded to daily requests for the association's library services department, providing publication information and resource referrals to association members and the public. I was also responsible for editing informational and promotional materials, as well as preparing for and working on-site at the association's annual international conference. As office support person for the ASPECT Foundation, I processed applications to the organization's study abroad program, distributed program materials to applicants, and used Microsoft Word and Excel extensively. These duties required strong communication skills, attention to detail, and an ability to both organize and prioritize several tasks at once.

I am very interested in education and the arts. At Bryn Mawr College, I took courses in both art and art history, and I participated in an educational exchange program through which I studied Renaissance art in Florence, Italy. Since then, I have taken extension courses through UC Berkeley in Asian and Latin American art history.

As a result of these experiences, I am enthusiastic about continuing to work with nonprofits, and would like to further explore career possibilities with public arts organizations. A position as Membership Assistant with the World Art Museum would combine my member services and clerical skills, my interests, and my career goals. I am confident I can be of value to your organization and the customers you serve. Please feel free to call me to set up an interview, or if you need more information. I look forward to hearing from you.

Sincerely,

Leticia Roberts

Enclosure

PERSONAL CONTACT

This letter is quick and to the point. The introduction can be brief, as the employer has already heard of the candidate through their mutual contact. Note that the employer is addressed by her first name; only do this if your contact has suggested it is appropriate. When in doubt, include the full name and title of your addressee.

Bill Pendleton
Address
City, state, zip code
Telephone
Email

June 14, 2003

Cathy Stevenson
McKinsey & Company
75 Park Plaza, 3rd Floor
Boston, MA 02116-3934

Dear Cathy,
Frank William suggested that I forward my resume to you for your consideration. I am a second-year MBA student at the Krannert Graduate School of Management at Purdue University, and I am currently working as a summer associate at Motorola in Chicago.

As Frank may have mentioned, I am in the top 5% of my class at Krannert, and I was recently elected president of the MBA student body. In and out of the classroom, I have consistently demonstrated my capacity to make a positive impact, regardless of the situation. My analytical and personal skills are ideally suited to management consulting, and I am confident that I would be an asset to McKinsey & Company.

I will call you next Wednesday to discuss next steps. If you have any questions regarding my resume or qualifications, please do not hesitate to call. I look forward to speaking with you.

Sincerely,

Bill Pendleton

Enclosure

BROADCAST LETTER

Linda emphasizes her personal qualities, as well as some of her background. This letter style is assertive, and will be most effective if she has done a good job researching the qualities this firm looks for in its candidates. The conclusion suggests a very proactive approach to targeting the prospective employer and requires follow-through.

LINDA S. BRADFORD
305 Locust Drive #12
Los Angeles, CA 90046
310-555-0883

August 30, 2000

Hamilton Trout
Andersen Consulting
Spear Street Tower
One Market Plaza
Suite 3700
San Francisco, CA 94105

Dear Hamilton:

I am writing to introduce myself as a candidate for a consulting position at your firm. I have excellent academic and professional credentials, as indicated on my enclosed resume. Throughout my professional career, I have adhered to the highest standards of excellence and have demonstrated strong communication skills, analytical ability, poise, creativity, and dedication.

Andersen's excellent reputation and corporate clientele are an ideal match with my interests and background. In particular, I believe my experience in formulating legal strategies and preparing analyses for complex litigation cases would be an excellent addition to your Strategic Services Competency Group.

I plan to be in San Francisco the week of September 15 and would like to meet with you then to further discuss my qualifications. I will call you on Friday and look forward to scheduling a meeting at your convenience in mid-September.

Very truly yours,

Linda S. Bradford

Contacting the Employer

Doing Your Due Diligence

Three Steps of Effective Research

Where to Look for Information

Before You Hit "Send"

Online Application Systems

Following Up

Thank-You Letters

Doing Your Due Diligence

Congratulations! You now have the tools to put together killer cover letters and resumes that are carefully gauged to appeal to each of the employers you are targeting in your job search. Of course, the next step is actually contacting prospective employers.

You may come to the job search armed with a great track record at work and school, numerous promotions and awards, and affiliations with prestigious institutions that most only dream of visiting. Or maybe this doesn't describe you at all, and you worry about how you will ever measure up. Whatever your background, you can be sure that you won't get far in the job market without doing your due diligence. A runner doesn't win the race without training, and a job seeker doesn't get an interview without laying some groundwork. Preparation, not impressive credentials, is the real key to success.

Good preparation begins with understanding the conditions and contexts of the job search. It's the difference between firing out resumes in great quantities with little focus, and taking a few well aimed shots directly at your desired targets. Your success rate will increase markedly if you do preliminary research before sending out your applications.

The essential role of research in your job search cannot be overemphasized. Recruiters and hiring managers consistently report that candidates who seem informed about the organization and the industry are given priority in the initial review of applications, and are most likely to succeed later at the interview stage. Almost every company will ask the question, "Why us?" Doing research ensures that you can answer this question in an educated fashion. You'll have a great advantage over your competition if you are able to express an understanding of the objectives of the organization (products, services, or operations), the company culture, and why your skills and experience are ideally suited to their needs.

WHY RESEARCH?

Imagine for a moment that you are the CEO of your dream company and want to hire one or more new employees. When you've got the pick of the litter, whom do you choose? Certainly you would want someone who's shown a genuine interest in your company by taking the time to learn about it and figure out how he or she could make it even better. Yes, your ideal future employee would take the job seriously, and perhaps even work for the company for years to come. Clearly the candidate who's done the research is going to get the interview call.

But it's not just for the employer's sake that you should research. To be genuinely enthusiastic, you need to know for yourself why the employer interests you. The company's primary industry, group, or specialty may be right in line with your career goals. Or you may be most excited by the company's standing in its field. Perhaps a discussion with a current employee about the company culture generates your interest. Every job and every company offer different opportunities for accomplishment; each will have various pros and cons. Do the research to clarify your own goals and priorities. Then use the information to find the right place in which you can succeed.

If the employer can't tell why you want the position and how you would benefit (besides the paycheck), they won't believe you are applying with serious intent. They will pass over your resume in favor of someone who has clearly articulated how his or her career goals will be furthered by the position. This is often why an "overqualified" candidate's application gets put into the "no" pile. Career changers and job searchers who are worried about appearing overqualified will benefit by stressing their goals for exposure to a new field. This approach allows candidates who have held a lot of responsibility in prior jobs to persuasively apply for a range of new positions. Whatever the case, make sure that your resume and cover letter accurately reflect your interests and show that you've done your homework.

One more time, with feeling: Before submitting a cover letter and resume to a potential employer, gather ammunition: information and insights (based on your research and self-assessment) that will target your "pitch" to exactly meet your prospective employer's goals.

Three Steps of Effective Research

The better the information you gather, the more on target your cover letter and resume will be. The key to successful investigation is knowing what to look for and where to find it. The following three steps will guide you through this all-important research process.

STEP 1: DECONSTRUCT THE JOB DESCRIPTION

When responding to a job posting, your application will be much more effective if it addresses the specific needs of the employer. A job description, included in any posting worth looking into, provides a great starting place to get a sense of the employer's desired skills and qualifications.

Begin by reading over the job description and noting any key words. Make a list of these, and as you revise your resume for the specific opening, include as many of these key words as possible. Now dig a little deeper to understand how you fit more specifically with the job description and how you can present this fit.

Ask yourself the following questions:

- How did you learn of the position opening? Through word-of-mouth or from an advertised job posting on a public source? (This will determine how you introduce yourself to the employer.)

- Who is the company trying to target as its source of qualified candidates? Do you belong in this pool of candidates? How do you stand out among them? (This can help you figure out how to differentiate yourself, while still addressing the needs of the employer.)

- Do you have an "in" from whom you can get the inside scoop about the firm's search? (Make some calls. Maybe a friend of a friend? Knowing the inside scoop can be the key to getting the attention of the right hiring manager.)

- Have you seen resumes of other professionals in the field? How similar or different are they from yours?

 **INSIDER TIP**

When responding to a posted job opening, make a list of significant key words included in the job description and be sure to include these in your resume and cover letter.

Now that you've sketched out some general information about the job and how you might fit into it, it's time to go a level deeper and analyze the posting for specifics that you can address point by point. Try your hand at the following exercise.

Analyzing a Job Description

Convincing employers that you have relevant qualifications greatly increases your chances for getting an interview. Respond to as much of the job listing as possible by creating a checklist of the employer's stated needs, and matching it as directly as possible to the statements in your cover letter and resume.

Have a look at the following sample, based on a real advertisement on an online job board. The italicized words form the basis for shaping your application materials.

Sports Marketing Internship

Are you interested in a *career in marketing*? Have you recently completed a marathon, triathlon, century ride or are you just an *avid sports participant*? We are looking for an *energetic, active* person to join our marketing team in a summer internship that will be rewarding, educational, and will provide all of the excitement of crossing the finish line after months of training!

About the internship:

The intern will *assist* in general marketing tasks from *program creation and implementation to preparing materials for programs/events.* He/she will help out with general *marketing office duties,* and will help out at field and in-store *events.* The marketing intern will have some in-store tasks as well, in order to *learn all aspects of marketing in a retail environment.* Some roles and responsibilities will fluctuate as help is needed in other areas.

Qualifications:

- *A background in marketing, with related experience*
- *An active lifestyle*
- *Excellent communication skills*
- *Outgoing and energetic (a "people" person)*
- *MS Office skills*
- *Illustrator*

About Our Company:

We are a *small, innovative, and growing company* with a retail store and an online site. We cater to athletes of all levels and provide the best brands in sports apparel at great prices. Our *grassroots marketing strategy* keeps us very well *connected* to the active community, and we are always on the go. However, we are much more than just a store with weekly programs and events geared toward *educating and benefiting our customers*. Our *team members are as active* as our customers, participating in events right next to them. For more information please see our website.

Schedule will be 20–30 hours a week, with some evening and/or weekend event work. You MUST have a *flexible* schedule!

Here's what the perfect candidate looks like:

Goals: career in marketing, learn about all aspects of retail marketing

Personal qualities: energetic, active, flexible, outgoing, good communicator, sports lover

Experiences that reflect the ability to: assist others, create, implement, serve at events, work as part of a team, use computers, understand sports

Interested in the company because: innovative, growing, customer-focused, team-oriented, energetic, and active environment

To demonstrate that your interests, goals, and skills are exactly what the employer is looking for, feel free to use the same words found in the job posting in your cover letter or resume. Synonyms work well, too.

PRACTICE ANALYZING A JOB DESCRIPTION

Now you give it a try. Print out a job posting that catches your eye. Highlight or circle the relevant words and phrases, and use them to fill in the spaces below.

Goals:

_____

_____

Personal qualities:

_____

_____

Experiences that reflect the ability to:

_____

_____

Interested in the company because:

_____

_____

STEP 2: CONTEMPLATE THE COMPANY

Look into the firm's noted areas of strength and focus to find out in which industries or product areas it excels. Make a list of these. Does any of your experience, education, or personal interests relate to these? Also, explore the following:

- How does this job support the other functions of the department, division, and overall organizational structure?

- What effect does the position have on other departments and what are their functions and structures?

- What are the company's stated goals and mission?

- What is the corporate culture?

- How stable is the company?

- Who are its competitors?

Gathering some answers to these questions will help you speak intelligently to the job description in your application, not to mention speak intelligently about the job if you get an interview. But also, and just as important, asking these questions from the beginning can help you surmise whether a job at this company is really suited to *you*, and addresses *your* career and workplace needs as well. Remember earlier when we talked about enthusiasm being an important factor in a successful job application? Well, if this is an opportunity that is really right for you, you probably can't help but exude some enthusiasm. If not, you should move on to something that better suites you.

STEP 3: INVESTIGATE THE INDUSTRY

Be sure to find and flesh out answers for the following:

- What are the latest developments in the field or industry?

- How is the current economy affecting the field?

- What trends are being forecast?

- How is the company you're interested in positioned in the industry?

Having some ideas about the overall industry to which you're applying can help you anticipate a few of the company's needs that aren't specifically stated in the job posting. Having the ability to address a job posting in the larger context of the industry will also show that you are serious about the job and view it from the stance of a professional. Recruiting and training new employees is expensive, and most employers hope that anyone they hire will stick around for a while. This also applies to entry-level and internship candidates who must show that they are serious enough to do more than just file papers and make copies.

All of this information should influence the way in which you construct your approach to the job search and how you choose to customize your resume and cover letter. The more knowledgeable you are, the clearer you will be about your potential role and the more you will impress employers with your ability to contribute to their organization. Without proper background research, your cover letter and resume will be a shot in the dark. You could get lucky, but why not illuminate the playing field?

 INSIDER TIP

Recruiters and hiring managers love it when candidates do their research because:

- The candidate does the legwork for the employer by pointing to the match between the candidate's qualifications and their needs.
- The candidate demonstrates knowledge of, and interest in, the company, putting his application ahead of the more generic ones that do not directly address the company's goals.
- The candidate's knowledge of the organization or company results in a higher likelihood of retention if hired, an advantage because it may preclude future costly and time-consuming replacement searches.

Where to Look for Information

The bottom line? The information that will make your resume and cover letter sparkle is out there; it's up to you to find it and make the most of it. Employer websites are a great place to start. Most provide instructions for submitting resumes and applying for jobs—this can help you determine how to focus your efforts in your application. To find out more about a specific employer, a position, or an industry, consult as many resources as are available to you. Go to the library, search the Web, call your dad, talk to your friends, attend networking events, contact your alma mater.

Here are some websites insiders recommend to jumpstart your investigation:

- To get in-depth information on some of the top hirers in the United States, check out WetFeet's Industry and Company Profiles (www.WetFeet.com).

- Catch up on the latest news about the company and industry you're interested in at PR Newswire (www.prnewswire.com), NewsDirectory.com, and the Business Times (www.bizjournals.com).

- America's Career InfoNet (brought to you by the U.S. Department of Labor) features helpful information on wages and employment trends (www.acinet.org).

- The Occupational Outlook Handbook from the U.S. Bureau of Labor Statistics (www.bls.gov/oco/home.htm) provides career and occupational information for various fields.

- WetFeet's Real People Profiles (www.WetFeet.com) provide an insider's view of day-to-day life in a wide range of fields.

NETWORKING

Nothing is better than having an "in" at the company where you're applying. Before you prepare your resume and cover letter, get in touch with someone who can help answer questions regarding what makes a good candidate. If you don't know someone on the "inside," try to make contact through personal networks or through professional associations.

You can find contact information on associations in almost every field or industry via the online directory provided by the American Society of Association Executives (www.asaenet.org) and the Internet Public Library's Database (www.ipl.org).

For more information on mastering the art of networking, consult the WetFeet Insider Guide *Networking Works!* Available at www.WetFeet.com

 **INSIDER TIP**

Top Five Things That Will Automatically Screen Out an Applicant

5. **Resume sent without indication of what you are applying for**

4. **Poor quality materials, including photocopies, handwritten, or typed applications**

3. **Not demonstrating the right qualifications for the position**

2. **Too many pages**

1. **Misspelling, poor editing, and bad grammar**

Before You Hit "Send"

Follow closely whatever instructions you have regarding sending your application, especially if you're responding to an online job listing. This piece of advice may sound basic, but a surprising number of candidates don't follow instructions and are automatically disqualified as a result. No one wants to hire a candidate who either can't follow instructions or doesn't pay attention.

Many, if not most, employers prefer to receive applications electronically, emailed directly or sent through the organization's human resources website. Make sure your efforts aren't derailed by technical difficulties after spending so much time crafting your excellent application materials. Follow the guidelines discussed earlier on creating an email cover letter, and keep these tips in mind when putting your email package together.

What's in a Name?

Name your resume document after yourself, not "Resume_2002.doc" but "R.Jones02.doc." This way, the recruiter or hiring manager can easily fish your document out of the sea of other resumes in his or her computer files.

Run the Spell Check

Errors in any type of written correspondence can get you dinged. Don't let the seeming informality of the electronic resume allow you to omit this key step.

But don't let your faith in technology make you complacent, either; spell checkers give all sorts of mistakes the green light. After you do the spell check, proofread it the old-fashioned way several times. Then get a friend or two to do it again.

Take It Out for a Test Drive

Email your resume to yourself, because you'd much rather it be you who catches technical problems and errors, and not a recruiter. Make sure the text looks right on the screen and prints out correctly.

You might also try emailing yourself at different accounts. Email accounts have different ways of reading things, and you don't want to take any chances that it will look messy when it reaches the recruiter's account.

Online Application Systems

A growing number of companies are now relying on online application systems to manage their inflow of job applicants. WetFeet's 2005 *Student Recruitment Report* found that approximately one third of the companies that candidates applied to required online applications. The National Association of Colleges and Employers *Job Outlook 2004 Winter Update* survey reported that 11.5 percent of employers who responded said that they plan to accept only online applications in the future. Clearly, use of online application systems is and will continue to be a growing trend, especially among larger companies. Job seekers need to be savvy about how these systems work and how to use them to their best advantage.

Many job seekers are wary of these online application systems because they perceive them as black holes, from which they receive no response whatsoever. They feel that the process is too impersonal to allow them to differentiate themselves amongst a virtually worldwide sea of candidates, and that they have better chances of landing an interview using alternative methods of contacting employers. This may be true if you have personal contacts inside a company—by all means, use them if you do—but you may actually be decreasing your chances of landing an interview by avoiding the online application.

Recruiters use these systems as their preferred method of managing job applications, and in many cases, applying online is the only way of getting in front of a company recruiter at all. Emailing or sending in a hard-copy resume may only prevent you from being viewed as a viable candidate. Recruiters may not have the time to enter your resume into the database themselves, meaning that you will not be included in their pool of candidates: those that show up in a search of their candidate database. So, while it certainly won't hurt to follow up your online application with an email (if that's even possible) or hard-copy resume, you should never avoid the online application process altogether.

HOW THEY WORK

Online application systems range in complexity, from one-page questionnaires asking for your contact information and allowing you to upload your resume as an attachment to multiple-page surveys asking detailed questions about your work experience, personal characteristics, and salary history. The system will then typically rate candidates' fit for a particular job according to how they answered these questions.

Once a candidate fills out an online application and submits it, she is added to the company's applicant database and is usually flagged or associated with the particular job to which she applied. That application is then available for other recruiters at the company to evaluate for any other job opportunities.

Not all online application systems work the same way. Some allow you to create a profile, which enables you to login and apply to various jobs at the company or upload your resume. Others may require you to reapply for each new job. It is very important that you know the rules of each system you're using. Read the instructions carefully and follow them. If something doesn't happen the way it should—for example, if you don't receive a follow-up email confirming your application when the system said that you should, reapply or follow up with the company to make sure your application went through. Technology snafus do happen with these online systems so it's important to know that if you're having trouble applying, try again or try at a later time. If you still have trouble getting your application to go through, then you should try to contact the company through an alternate method, explaining, of course, why you're doing so.

BE THOROUGH AND THOUGHTFUL

Don't fall into the black-hole mentality. Recruiters really are on the other end looking at your responses and evaluating them, so it's crucial that you thoughtfully answer each and every question the system asks you. Many candidates simply submit their resumes without taking the time to answer the additional screening questions, believing them to be a waste of time. But this is a mistake. You should always answer each question carefully to show that you really are interested in the job opportunity and are willing to provide the information necessary to evaluate you.

And alternately, if the system requires you to fill out all of your job experience and qualifications in text fields, but also allows you to upload your resume as a document, do it. Cover all your bases and complete each step.

BE HONEST

Candidates give themselves the best chances of getting noticed, and being matched to the right job, if they answer all of the application questions truthfully. It may be tempting to click all of the answers you think recruiters might be looking for, but doing so is only a disservice to you, and a waste of your and the recruiter's time. If it turns out that you're really not qualified for the job, you'll be screened out during the interview process anyway, or worse, get hired for a job that you aren't qualified for, setting yourself up for a grand failure.

KEY IN ON KEYWORDS

Many of these candidate management systems use keywords to conduct searches. When a recruiter does an electronic search for a candidate, the results are ranked by the number of times the keywords searched for are found in the resumes listed. You'll give yourself the best chances of turning up in a recruiter's search, or ranking closer to the top of a recruiter's candidate list for a certain job, if you use words in your application that are derived from the job description or the company's website.

Examples of keywords include: Microsoft, product management, SQL Server, HR, human resources, communication skills, MBA, technical writer, data delivery, administrative assistant, developing, creating.

Some recruiters suggest placing a "key skills" section at the top of your resume that lists all of the keywords relevant to the particular job, separated by commas or periods. (This only applies to resumes submitted to these types of databases.) If you choose to try this technique, keep your summary between 20 and 30 items.

Other keyword tricks include using different forms of the same keyword. For example, if you used "coordination" in your skills summary, use "coordinate" in the body of your resume. Using different keyword forms will maximize your ranking in a recruiter's search. Also, use both complete-word keywords and acronyms. For example, your resume should include both "MBA" and "Masters of Business Administration," or both "HR" and "Human Resources." Try to cover all your bases.

WHAT ABOUT A COVER LETTER?

In many cases, the online application system will prompt you with open-ended questions (such as "What most qualifies you for the XYZ position?") followed by a text field for your customized response. In many cases these customized responses can serve the purpose of your cover letter by allowing you to differentiate yourself. In other cases, a text field in which you can paste your cover letter precedes the resume attachment function, or you may be allowed to upload more than one attachment. If that option is not available, many candidates simply include their cover letter with their resume in the same document. If you do this, be sure to add a page break between your cover letter and resume so that your formatting is intact and the entire package is more presentable.

Following Up

What a relief! The writing, editing, and proofreading are finally over. The documents have been sent. Anticipation tingles up and down your spine as you daydream about the call you'll get from the employer. Think you can relax? Think again. Support all that hard work by following through with an additional step. If you really, truly want the job, continue to show your interest *after* you have sent the application.

Place a phone call or send an email to confirm your materials were received and to reiterate your desire to learn more about the position. Don't become a nuisance, but do be persistent. After all, many employers look for people who take initiative and are good problem solvers.

Follow these basic guidelines for constructive follow-up, and you won't go wrong:

- **Be persistent but not pesky.** Two calls in one day are overkill; two calls in one week are probably fine.

- **Be prescriptive in your requests.** Ask specifically for what you want, whether it's to ensure that the prospective employer has received your resume, to schedule an interview, or to have a casual chat on the phone.

- **Keep the ball in your court.** You'll probably feel more in control if you can plan the next steps rather than wait by the phone.

- **Make yourself easily available.** Provide a number where a message can be left at any time.

Employers say that at this early stage, there is a fine line between the interested candidate and the pesky one. But the hiring staff we interviewed unanimously said it couldn't hurt and could most definitely help your application if you take some time to follow up by contacting them in a respectful manner—a few calls or emails, and *that's it.*

If you need guidance on what to say, try adapting one of these scripts:

> "This is Kelly Purcell. I sent you an application for the EMT position a few days ago and am following up to ensure that you received my materials. Please let me know if you have any questions. If you are available to discuss my qualifications at greater length, I would like to schedule an interview. I can be reached today at 555-444-5555. On Thursday and Friday, it's best to call my cell phone, 555-657-6699. I'm looking forward to the chance to speak with you directly."

OR

> "This is Merrill Morgan calling on Wednesday. I'm an MBA candidate from Fuqua with experience in the M&A group at UBS. At John Smith's request, I sent my resume to you on Monday. I would like to schedule an interview and will call you on Friday to discuss my qualifications."

In the latter script, the candidate leaves a brief message with some information on his background so the associate or recruiter will remember seeing the resume. He is specific about his plans to call back on Friday, which gives him an opportunity to inform John Smith that he followed up on his request.

If you've left three messages and all have been ignored, you may want to send your resume to someone else at the organization and try the process again. Many firms communicate primarily through voice mail, although you might have luck using email or even leaving a good old-fashioned message with the receptionist. Tailor your approach to what you've learned about how that particular company communicates.

Thank-You Letters

Say that all your hard work, your customized cover letter and tailored resume, has led you to a meeting with an employer. Your research into the company and your own background helped you have a smooth and convincing interview. Or maybe the interview went pretty well, but there were a few points you wish you had made differently. (We've all been there!)

The thank-you letter is another tool you can use to add extra oomph to your candidacy. Short and sweet, this note shows gratitude for the time the employer has taken to review your qualifications, and it's an opportunity to demonstrate (again) that you are clearer than ever in your understanding of the fit between the position and your qualifications and goals. The thank-you letter has a bonus function, too: It gives you a final opportunity to address any weakness or clarify any misunderstanding that may have occurred in the interview process. The sample thank-you letter we've included mentions specifics of the meeting, shows appreciation, and reminds the employer of the candidate's strengths.

SAMPLE EMAILED THANK-YOU LETTER

RE: Coordinator, Member Services – 2/26 Interview

February 27, 2003

Janet Lewis, Executive Director New York Global

Dear Janet,

I genuinely enjoyed meeting with you yesterday and learning more about New York Global and the clients you serve. I believe strongly that helping immigrants utilize their skills and training in a well-matched work environment is beneficial for both the individuals and the U.S. employers who hire them. I find the goals of your organization, in offering both direct services and advocacy on the issue of workforce diversity, admirable.

I was glad to be able to answer some of your questions regarding my background, approach to client services, and career goals. After our discussion, I continue to be eager to support the mission of New York Global and believe I could make a significant contribution as Coordinator of Member Services. In particular, my prior experience creating and delivering workforce diversity trainings and resources, along with my knowledge of local employers (developed through professional experience and through personal contacts as a native New Yorker) could serve your organization as you seek to build and strengthen client programming and outreach.

Please let me know if you have further questions, would like more information, or would like a list of my professional references. Feel free to contact me at your convenience via email or telephone at (212) 555-1212. I look forward to hearing from you.

Sincerely,

Rachel Hertz, M.A.

rachelhertz@hotmail.com

For Your Reference

Recommended Resources

Books

Surveys

Author Bios

Recommended Resources

The resources that follow represent some of the best tools in developing job search materials. They correspond to suggestions we've made in this guide about preparation through research, and also provide access to more resume and cover letter information and samples. However, be aware that this is but a small sampling of the information that's available to help you effectively develop killer cover letters and resumes. So use the following as a jumping-off point in your research endeavors and feel free to explore the vast array of information that's out there on this topic.

RESUMES AND LETTERS

- Get resume feedback from a career or resume advisor. Most university career centers offer free resume consultations or workshops for students, and for alumni at a nominal fee.

- Check out WetFeet's website for resume advice at www.WetFeet.com.

- Have a look at the Riley Guide, which comprises an extensive compilation of links to information on writing resumes and cover letters, as well as other useful job search information (www.rileyguide.com).

RESEARCHING EMPLOYERS

- Use Google or another Internet search engine to find a company or organization's website (www.google.com).

- WetFeet Company Profiles give crucial insider information on top companies, including key indicators for success such as annual revenue, employee hiring numbers, and latest trends (www.WetFeet.com).

- NewsDirectory.com or the *Business Times* (www. bizjournals.com) can help you in your search for current information on companies, organizations, and industry news.

RESEARCHING THE POSITION

- The Occupational Outlook Handbook from the Bureau of Labor Statistics contains valuable information on occupational paths. Learn about qualifications, trends, and related occupations at http://www.bls.gov/oco/home.htm.

- WetFeet's Real People Profiles can give you a better understanding about the ins and outs of a variety of professions, and what it takes to succeed in them (www.WetFeet.com).

- Salary.com features searchable salary information by career categories and by location. Use this information to research and respond to salary expectation questions (www.salary.com).

- Job market and hiring trend information from NACE (National Association of Colleges and Employers) can keep you up to date on your job search (www.jobweb.com).

INDUSTRIES AND FIELDS

- The U.S. Department of Labor's America's Career InfoNet can give you a sense of the bigger picture on wages and employment trends (http://www.acinet.org/acinet/default.asp?tab=wagesandtrends).

- WetFeet Industry Profiles provide a fairly in-depth view of what it's like to work in various industries from accounting to venture capital (www.WetFeet.com).

- Search information on associations in almost every field or industry via online directories: the American Society of Association Executives (www.asaenet.org/GeneralDetail.cfm?ItemNumber=1796) and the Internet Public Library's Database (www.ipl.org/div/aon).

- Associations often have useful industry and career path information on their websites, and contacting members can be a great way to network—one of the best sources of insider information for your job search.

Books

Your Rights in the Workplace

Barbara Kate Repa (Nolo Press)
This book does a good job of informing readers about their rights and responsibilities as future employees.

Gallery of Best Cover Letters:
A Collection of Quality Cover Letters by Professional Resume Writers

David Noble (JIST Works)
This provides valuable cover letter samples across a wide spectrum of industries, and with a wide variety of styles.

WetFeet Insider Guides

WetFeet's Insider Guides give you real insight into the industries and employers that interest you most. Check out the additional titles available at www.WetFeet.com to assist you with your job search. You'll find guides that focus on everything from how to network, ace your interviews, and negotiate a good salary.

Surveys

Here's more information about the two surveys cited in this book:

ResumeDoctor.com provides expert advice to job seekers, employers, and members of the media. ResumeDoctor.com is a subsidiary of Personal Department Inc. (PDI), Vermont's largest independently owned staffing agency. For more information, go to www.ResumeDoctor.com.

Since 1956, the **National Association of Colleges and Employers** (NACE) has been the leading source of information about the employment of college graduates. The *Job Outlook 2005* report forecasts the hiring intentions of employers and examines other issues related to the employment of new college graduates. NACE surveyed its employer members for the *Job Outlook 2005* report from mid-August through September 30, 2004; it is one of four NACE reports for the 2004 to 2005 academic year. Other reports for 2004 to 2005 include the *Job Outlook 2005 Fall Preview*, released in September 2005; the *Job Outlook 2005 Winter Update*, published in December 2004; and the *Job Outlook 2005 Spring Update*, published in April 2005. For more information, check out www.naceweb.com.

Author Bios

Rosanne Lurie, M.S., has been a career advisor in the Bay Area for more than six years, at public and private institutions, including University of California, San Francisco, and University of California, Berkeley. Her professional background includes career advising through individual counseling and workshops, as well as developing and managing online and print resources for career center websites and libraries. In addition to orienting undergrads to career planning, she has worked with graduate students and alumni to develop their job searching skills for academic, clinical, and industry positions. A San Francisco native, she attended Haverford College near Philadelphia and earned a master's degree in counseling from San Francisco State University. As a career advisor, she enjoys helping her clients choose their career direction and pursue their life goals.

Selena Welz, WetFeet's senior editor, has worked with a vast array of career subjects, including interviewing skills, conducting job research, negotiating salaries and perks, and, of course, writing cover letters and resumes. In addition, she has studied and written extensively on various career paths, ranging from investment banking to engineering to fine arts and graphic design. Selena tracks current career, recruiting, and workplace trends for job seekers, reporting regularly on WetFeet's weblog (www.wetfeet.com/Content/WebLog.aspx). A graduate of the University of California, Berkeley, Selena lives and works in San Francisco.

WETFEET'S INSIDER GUIDE SERIES

Job Search Guides

Getting Your Ideal Internship

International MBA Student's Guide to the U.S. Job Search

Job Hunting A to Z: Landing the Job You Want

Killer Consulting Resumes!

Killer Cover Letters & Resumes!

Killer Investment Banking Resumes!

Negotiating Your Salary & Perks

Networking Works!

Interview Guides

Ace Your Case: Consulting Interviews

Ace Your Case II: 15 More Consulting Cases

Ace Your Case III: Practice Makes Perfect

Ace Your Case IV: The Latest & Greatest

Ace Your Case V: Return to the Case Interview

Ace Your Case VI: Mastering the Case Interview

Ace Your Interview!

Beat the Street: Investment Banking Interviews

Beat the Street II: I-Banking Interview Practice Guide

Career & Industry Guides

Careers in Accounting

Careers in Advertising & Public Relations

Careers in Asset Management & Retail Brokerage

Careers in Biotech & Pharmaceuticals

Careers in Brand Management

Careers in Consumer Products

Careers in Entertainment & Sports

Careers in Health Care

Careers in Human Resources

Careers in Information Technology

Careers in Investment Banking

Careers in Management Consulting

Careers in Marketing & Market Research

Careers in Nonprofits & Government Agencies

Careers in Real Estate

Careers in Retail

Careers in Sales

Careers in Supply Ch

Careers in Venture C

Industries & Careers

Industries & Careers

Million Dollar Care

Specialized Consulti
and Information Te

Company Guide

25 Top Consulting F

25 Top Financial Ser

Accenture

Bain & Company

Booz Allen Hamilton

Boston Consulting C

Credit Suisse First B

Deloitte Consulting

Deutsche Bank

The Goldman Sachs

J.P. Morgan Chase &

McKinsey & Comp

Merrill Lynch & Co.

Morgan Stanley

WetFeet in the City Guides

Job Hunting in New York City

Job Hunting in San Francisco